PSYCHIC DREAMOLOGY

the text of this book is printed on 100% recycled paper

PSYCHIC DREAMOLOGY

Norvell

BARNES & NOBLE BOOKS
A DIVISION OF HARPER & ROW, PUBLISHERS
New York, Hagerstown, San Francisco, London

 For information address Harper & Row, Publishers, Inc., 10 East 53d Street, New York, N. Y. 10022. Published simultaneously in Canada by Fitzhenry & Whiteside Limited, Toronto.

First BARNES & NOBLE BOOKS edition published 1977

LIBRARY OF CONGRESS CATALOG CARD NUMBER: 76–21167

INTERNATIONAL STANDARD BOOK NUMBER: 0–06–464017–5
77 78 79 80 81 5 4 3 2 1

CONTENTS

PSYCHIC DREAMOLOGY

INTRODUCTION

Since time immemorial, man has been mystified by his dreams. But he has felt that somehow dreams expressed some higher power within his own mind trying to warn him of coming events or revealing a pattern of destiny known only to this power.

Shakespeare wrote of this mystical dimension of time and space, beyond the ordinary everyday experiences of conscious mental activity:

We are such stuff
As dreams are made on; and our little life
Is rounded with a sleep.

Modern psychologists think that there is more to dreaming than was formerly believed by Freud and his followers, who felt that dreams represented suppressed desires mostly associated with the sexual instinct.

Some psychologists have come to the conclusion that dreams represent another dimension in which extrasensory powers are released by a higher, superconscious mind, that this mind is trying to weave a tapestry of dreams to reveal a pattern of destiny that the dreamer himself has chosen. In this way the dreamer senses his future in symbolical form by actually tapping his own higher psychic senses. Most people who have had psychic or clairvoyant dreams undoubtedly tapped this superconscious mind and in some mysterious fashion were made aware of events that were to occur.

WHAT IS THIS OTHER DIMENSION OF DREAMS?

Mystics have long believed that the soul, the higher consciousness in man, has its own separate domain in which it is able to project itself backwards or forwards in time and space. When the dreamer awakes and remembers his dreams, he is confronted by an experience that occurred in another dimension of time but that may have vital information to reveal about his future life experiences.

Dr. Joseph Rhine of Duke University tells of a young woman who dreamed that her brother had hanged himself in the loft of his barn. She awakened her husband, and they drove to her brother's house. They saw a light in the loft of the barn, and upon entering it, they found her brother hanging from a rafter!

Joan of Arc had prophetic and clairvoyant dreams; they revealed to her that she would lead the armies of France to victory. When these dreams came true, many church leaders believed that she was a witch and that the devil had revealed these accurate events to her.

In this book I shall give you the results of many years of investigation into psychic phenomena connected with clairvoyance, clairaudience, ESP, precognition, and other forms of extrasensory perception that I have personally investigated. I am convinced that we can tap the power of this higher mind, and harness it to work for us. By knowing how to use Psychic Dreamology, you may expect the following results:

1. You will discover another dimension of soul-awareness that works while you sleep and that can reveal many mysteries to you through your dreams.
2. You will learn how to analyze your dreams by knowing the universal language of mystical symbols that your higher mind uses to reveal the pattern of future events.

3. You can actually use your dream to project what you wish to experience in your real life. By a method that you will learn, you can project events on the psychic screen of your higher mind and make these events come true. In this way you can program the higher psychic mind to the work you wish to do, the money you want to make, the romantic partner you want to attract, the house you wish to live in, the friends you want—and then you can actually dream these desires into existence!

4. You can use the dream world to act out your own life fantasies, thereby ridding yourself of complexes, guilt feelings, self-consciousness, and feelings of inferiority and inadequacy. You can project into these fantasies the past events that have caused you problems and then act out any role that you choose to make these fantasies into the reality that fits your needs and that brings emotional security and the fulfillment of your life destiny.

5. Through your dreams you can receive instruction from the cosmic mind that knows all, sees all, and is all-powerful. Many artists have learned how to paint from these dream "Masters" who projected on their psychic screens the actual pictures that they later reproduced on their canvasses. One composer of popular music who has made millions through his songs admits that he receives not only his ideas but also actual words and music while he is on the dream plane. When he awakes, he still hears the songs ringing in his ears, which he then transfers to paper. He says that this method of composing is much better than when he had to cudgel his conscious mind for ideas, words, and music.

Many great composers of the past used this same technique. Mozart said that his beautiful music came to him "out of the air," seeming to indicate that even when he was awake some higher creative intelligence was at work, bringing his music from another dimension of consciousness.

6. You can learn another language or develop some gift like writing stories or inventing useful objects by programming your higher "dream consciousness" to these creative tasks just before you go to sleep at night.

7. You can receive clairvoyant and clairaudient prophecies of future events, in which you may have a preview peek at your fu-

ture destiny, glimpse the face of your future mate, or receive warnings of accidents, tragedies, or disasters, which you may be able to avoid. Dreams can reveal the pattern of events that are still in the future dimensions of time and space but which are revealed on the dream plane.

A man dreamed that the daily double would come in on a certain racetrack, with a certain number being shown the winner. He followed his dream hunch and made $35,000.

Emanuel Swedenborg, the noted eighteenth-century mystic, reported that he received a vision of a fire 300 miles away, while he sat meditating in a dreamlike state. Later, this fire was confirmed as having actually occurred while he was having his vision!

8. You can indulge in astral flights, vivid, dreamlike states in which the soul seems to explore other dimensions of time and space. You can revisit historical sites of past ages; you can become an actor in ancient dramas like the sacking of Rome, the building of the pyramids, the glories of Greece in its Golden Age of philosophy, drama, poetry, and politics. You can let your dreams carry you to other planets and to new worlds beyond the limits of today's knowledge into spiritual dimensions of cosmic soul-awareness that reveal secrets of the universe.

Robert Louis Stevenson confessed that he wrote most of his stories while in a dreamlike state, as his characters paraded across his consciousness, speaking, acting, and living out their life dramas before his very eyes.

I once interviewed Margaret Mitchell, who wrote *Gone With the Wind,* and she told me that she dreamed up most of her characters and events while she slept, and when awake she merely transferred these mental and visual images to paper.

9. Dreams can help you solve your problems and reveal methods for achieving your goals and aspirations. In a dream you can try and discard hundreds of ideas, and then when the right solution comes along, your conscious mind will wake you up and cause you to remember it. In this way you have access to hidden information that your superconscious mind knows.

Thomas A. Edison used this psychic dream technique to find the right materials for his electric light filament. He had tried thousands of different substances when he finally received the solution to that problem in a vivid dream. He awakened and wrote it down, and the next morning he found out that it worked perfectly.

10. Dreams are often used by your unconscious to mask events that cause distress, frustration, rage, and rebellion in your daily life. Suppressing these feelings can lead to disquieting experiences in your work and in your relationships with friends, your mate, your children, and others. By knowing the various disguises that your unconscious takes in your dreams, you can ferret out these painful events and remove them completely from your subconscious and thus from your life.

11. You can utilize your dreams to make a reality of your love fantasies. It is in dreams that your unconscious reveals sexual patterns that may be abhorrent to your waking, conscious mind and that are hidden in your love relations with the opposite sex. This conflict often leads to problems of frigidity in women and premature ejaculation in men or inability to perform the sex act. Your dreams will be an accurate guage of your suppressed sexual desires, and you can then act realistically to bring these fantasies into line with reality, making you a more complete human being with a satisfactory sex life.

12. You can often discover your hidden talents and potential for greatness through your dream revelations. When your unconscious keeps repeating a dream in which you are singing, acting, dancing, painting, composing music, writing stories, or inventing objects, it might be pointing the way to a natural talent that has long been suppressed by your conscious mind. By following this lead, you can often be guided to the development of gifts that could make your fortune or bring you great personal satisfaction.

13. Are you one who dreams perpetually of sickness, accidents, tragedies, murder, theft, rape, crimes of passion, and violence? Such dreams can become a source of great unhappiness to a person who does not know the true symbology of dreams.

A fourteen-year-old boy kept having a dream in which he stabbed his grandmother to death with a butcher's knife. He could not understand this frightening dream, for he loved his grandmother. He told no one of his dream. One day, passing through the kitchen, he saw his grandmother working at the stove and a butcher's knife on a nearby table. Some impulse made him grab the knife and stab his grandmother to death! This tragic fulfillment of his dream could have been avoided if he had consulted with a psychologist or his parents about his troubling dream. The dream might have indicated suppressed rage at his parents' discipline that he took out on his grandmother, because his higher mind could not project killing his own mother and father.

14. Discover the secret power of commanding and controlling others through the dream world. Mystics believe that when we sleep the soul has a life of its own. Even Dr. Rhine came to the conclusion that ESP and mental telepathy might utilize some higher power to project thought forms. Through dreams at night you can reach out into the astral realms and project your thoughts into the minds of others.

A woman dreamed herself into her husband's mind and projected that he would tell her if he was having an affair with a woman she suspected. Two nights later the husband turned to her and voluntarily confessed he was having such an affair.

Dream yourself into your boss's mind and tell him you want a raise. Dream your way into important people's lives and ask them for favors, loans, or gifts of value. Use your dreams for influencing others to love you and to help you.

15. Your dreams can often guide you to hidden money or the finding of lost objects or other valuable things. A man dreamed that money was hidden in an upholstered chair in a neighbor's house. Upon investigation, he found $92,000 there.

A lawyer lost a valuable paper that he needed in a case coming up for trial. He could not find the paper anywhere. He projected the wish to his unconscious that it would guide him to finding the paper. In his dream he saw himself going to his filing cabinet where he searched and finally found the paper. When he awoke, he remembered that he had already searched the cabinet without success. However, the next day at his office, he looked again and this time found the paper, which had somehow become caught and had lodged in the upper part of the cabinet where it could not be seen.

These and many more amazing things can be revealed by your dreams. Study this book thoroughly, digesting all the information carefully, and then utilize this knowledge to program your own subconscious mind with the information you wish to obtain from your dreams. You can also check the list of universal symbols (page 157) to find out what your dreams mean from a psychological viewpoint and then act accordingly to rid yourself of bad habits, inferiority complexes, problems, failure syndromes, or other qualities that you wish to rid yourself of.

1

HOW TO TAP THE PSYCHIC POWER OF YOUR DREAMS AND MAKE THEM WORK FOR YOU

Most people dream at least once during every ninety minutes of sleep. Scientists have discovered in laboratory tests that the average person in a normal sleep period of eight hours is likely to have as many as six dreams. Even people who boast that they never dream have frequent dreams, but they do not recall them because their unconscious has some reason for concealing them.

In leading universities and research centers throughout the country, scientists have been working for many years to discover the mystery of dreams. A great deal more is known about this other dimension of time and space than was known in Freud's time. Now we know that dreams have significance if we are able to interpret them.

There are prophetic dreams that actually seem to tap another stratum of cosmic time to project the dreamer into a future dimension that has not yet been born.

Jules Verne, who in the nineteenth century accurately dreamed of 200 modern inventions like the submarine, television, radio, space ships, and airplanes, had a type of clairvoyant dream that actually showed him the world of the future.

There are dreams that occur frequently that seem to reveal a mystical pattern that the dreamer cannot fathom unless he is versed in the science of dreamology. When these dreams are understood, he will know that the unconscious is trying to point out something vitally important that has been concealed from the dreamer in his conscious existence.

Someone once said, "A dream is a wish your heart makes." Your unconscious mind often projects your real desires and hopes in the form of dreams, knowing that the conscious mind might reject them as being unattainable or ridiculous.

A country girl who lived in the Midwest, far from cultural centers, kept dreaming that she was a singer at the Metropolitan Opera House in New York City. When she suppressed this dream, she became miserable and felt she had to tell someone. She finally confided it to her mother, who was sympathetic and found a singing teacher for her. The girl's dream was indeed prophetic, for the teacher discovered that she really had a good voice. After she had studied for a few years, the townspeople raised a fund to send her to New York City where she began training with an opera coach. In a short time this country girl became a star at the Metropolitan Opera House! She was Marion Talley, and she confided this secret to me once when I interviewed her in her dressing room at the old Met.

PSYCHIC AND CLAIRVOYANT DREAMS

Your dreams can be psychic and clairvoyant, trying to reveal something to you about the future or guide you to certain actions in order to fulfill your destiny.

Time is a mysterious element that man has compartmented and labeled "past, present, and future." According to Einstein, this stream of time is relative and depends on one's orientation in time and space. If the dream state is actually an acceleration of this stream of time, perhaps dreams become prophetic and portray events that have not yet come into being.

Just as a child is the genetic expression of his mother and father and is projected into being even before conception takes place, so too the dream images that we conjur at night are reflections of our brain children that will fashion themselves into a reality from the dream tapestry we have unconsciously woven.

In this way we can truly say that the Oriental mystics were accurate in their appraisal of what goes on in our dream states. A legend from the Far East typifies this insight. An ancient king went out from the palace gates and rode at the head of his troops each day. One morning he saw a beggar asking for alms, and the king threw him a coin. Then he stopped and asked the man, "Tell me, why are you a beggar?" The beggar thought for a moment and then replied, "It is true, your Highness, by day I am a beggar, but at night, in my dreams I am a king. Whereas, you, your Highness, are a king by day, but at night in your dreams you fear becoming the beggar I am. Who then is really a beggar and who is king?"

Almost every millionaire dreams of losing his millions and awakes in a cold sweat at the thought of facing such stark reality. Our unconscious minds have the task of censoring us, reminding us of what tragedies can befall us, and presenting all this in dreams and nightmares that seem all too frighteningly real.

You can learn how to program your higher psychic mind centers with the dreams that you want to make into living reality.

You can also project to this higher mind a pattern of events that will arrange themselves logically in your dreams and give you a preview of that future destiny you are creating.

You can tell this higher psychic mind, which stems from the superconscious realm, that you want it to solve your problems while you sleep. In a strange and mysterious fashion this higher mind will project dreams to solve your problems perfectly.

However, as the unconscious often works in universal symbols, it may mask its true intent and purpose in symbology, which you will learn to interpret in this book.

You can enter into the dream world while you sleep at night and ask to be given psychic and clairvoyant dreams that will show you how to get the money you need, find the right job for you, heal your body, meet your true soul mate—you name it and this hidden genie of your unconscious must create the drama for you, cast you as its leading star, people it with characters of your own choosing, and act it out against a backdrop that you yourself select. You not only become the main actor in this dream drama, but you also write the lines you are to speak, make the costumes you wear, and choose the other characters who appear with you.

You also have the power to make this playacting of your dreams a comedy, a drama of tragedy and suffering, a romantic episode in which you are the lover or the beloved, or a melodrama in which impossible things occur. The choice is all up to you, for you are setting the dream-stage for acting out your own psychic visions of the future.

HOW TO TAP THE PSYCHIC POWER OF YOUR DREAMS

1. Just before you go to bed each night, have a session with your unconscious, sometimes called the subconscious. You can make out a dream schedule on which you list some of the things you want your psychic centers to project through your dreams. Your dream schedule can include anything you desire. I am giving samples here of what some people might want for their dream schedules, but you may choose others.

I wish to have clairvoyant and psychic visions of the following things that I desire in my life. I ask that psychic guidance come to me through my dreams, revealing the pattern of my future destiny.

I wish to be shown how I can make $100,000 safely and without great effort.

I want an invention that can make me famous and rich.

I ask for the solution to my marriage problem: Should I get a divorce or should I stay married?

I wish to know who my true soul mate is to be. I wish to have a precognitive vision in every detail of the person I shall marry.

I desire to become a public personality. (Here you can state if you wish to be an actor, singer, dancer, TV director, designer, cosmologist, or any other creative role you desire.)

I wish to be shown a psychic picture of my future home, where I shall live, and how I can obtain this home.

2. After you have written down such a dream schedule, listing what you want your higher psychic mind to project in your

dreams, read it over once or twice and be sure that it reflects accurately the things that you really want.

Then lie down and prepare for your usual sleep, with this exception: Instead of forcing yourself to go to sleep, start to mentally review each event that you have listed on your dream schedule. Make yourself the main actor in each incident of that dream schedule, seeing yourself living it fully. As you progress down the list, you will find yourself becoming very drowsy, and soon you will fall asleep. This, by the way, is an excellent cure for insomnia.

Robert H. learned of this technique from a lesson I had on dreamology in our lecture work in Los Angeles. He needed $50,000 to open a business that he had long planned. As he had exhausted all other sources for raising the money, he decided to give the problem to his higher psychic mind. When he went to bed each night, he kept programming the thought, "I need $50,000 to open my own business. I ask my higher psychic mind to show me a way by which I can raise that money." He then visualized the place of business he desired, pictured his name on the store front, and mentally saw customers flocking into his store. He finally drifted off to sleep and his psychic centers were now programmed with one overwhelming thought: *Show me how to get the sum of $50,000*.

One night he had a vivid dream in which he saw himself at the Santa Anita Racetrack betting on the horses. This in itself was surprising, for he seldom gambled. He saw numbers one and one in the daily double, and he awoke with the vivid feeling that he must go to the racetrack. The next day he took $100 and followed his psychic hunch, betting it all on number one in the first and second races.

The two horses he selected were long shots at the odds of 35 to 1. He felt that they could never win against the favorites, but he went ahead and bought the tickets anyway. In the first race his horse trailed the field until the stretch when it suddenly began to surge ahead, winning by a half a length!

In the second race his horse was second all the way around the track, and at the finish line the favorite seemed to be ahead. The man's heart sank, and he was about to tear up his tickets when

PHOTO FINISH flashed on the big board, and he realized that he still had a chance to win. After a tense few moments, number one flashed onto the board as the winner, and he knew that his clairvoyant and psychic dream had been accurate. This man won $35,000 from his tickets, and with this sum he was able to go into the business he had long dreamed of opening.

3. In order to prepare your subconscious to receive your dreams and project them to your conscious mind when you awake, just before you go to sleep prepare your mental psychic screen, on which you project various pictures of things you want to dream into existence.

Mentally visualize a motion picture screen that stretches across your forehead but that is inside your head. Onto this psychic screen you will now practice by projecting thought forms and pictures of the things you are asking your dream-self to bring you. For example, "I wish to know my true soul mate." Now mentally project various types of faces onto the screen, making up your own images or using composites of people you know or famous personalities you admire. As this picture keeps flashing onto your psychic screen, you are sensitizing your higher psychic centers to do the identical thing in your dream world. In this way you will soon acquire proficiency in making your dreams more vivid and detailed.

Man in the South Pacific Dreamed His Soul Mate into Existence

A lieutenant in the South Pacific during World War II once dreamed that he had found his true soul mate, a beautiful girl who perfectly matched the picture he had always envisioned of his dream girl. One day in looking through a movie magazine, he was shocked to see his dream girl; she was a famous movie star and it was way beyond any possibility that he would ever meet her, much less marry her.

He cut out that picture, framed it, and put it beside his bed. Every night just before he drifted off to sleep, he kissed his dream girl and promised himself, "I shall meet you one day and you will fall in love with me and marry me." In his dreams he had fantasies in which his dream girl became real, married him, bore him children, and settled with him in a home in the San Fernando Valley.

A few weeks later, this man found himself in San Francisco on leave for a week. He met a friend who invited him to a big party and dance on Nob Hill. He wore his white summer uniform, and when he walked into the large living room of his host's home, the orchestra was playing a waltz. Across the room from him, as if in a dream, he saw a beautiful girl drifting towards him. She floated into his arms, and they danced together, not even knowing each other's name. That night, *before the party ended,* he proposed to the girl of his dreams, and she accepted him! It seemed to both of them that they had known each other for a lifetime. The girl's name was Ruth Hussey. She and the young officer were later married, settled down in the San Fernando valley, and had their family—exactly as the lieutenant had seen it happening on his mind's psychic screen in his prophetic dream!

4. In sensitizing your mental psychic screen, project the particular gifts and talents you wish to develop, and each night when you go to sleep, see yourself, for example, composing songs, writing stories, or inventing objects.

A woman who did this had studied dreamology at one of my classes, and she made up her mind she wanted to make money through inventions. She projected this thought to her mental psychic screen and tried to devise new products that might bring her a fortune. One night she had a vivid dream of how an extra cake of soap could be made from tiny pieces of leftover soap, which were put into a plastic dish shaped like a bar of soap, and later solidified. She awakened and jotted down her idea, which she later developed and sold to a manufacturer in Chicago.

5. Give yourself a dream catharsis. Many people's psychic centers are clouded by distorted and disorganized dreams that have a way of returning night after night to plague the dreamer. This is often due to the mental programming we receive all our lives. Dream catharsis will help remove these negative mental images from your subconscious and return you to a wholesome, free state, where you will no longer have nightmares and dreams of sickness, accident, death, tragedy, and other misfortune.

This is one of the reasons why most psychiatrists and psychologists ask their patients to tell them of their dreams. The doctor is able to get a clue to the programming of the patient's subconscious mind and then through a system of mental catharsis, known as psychotherapy, the doctor is able to reprogram the person's mind with healthy, wholesome, and pleasant experiences.

You can do this type of dream catharsis yourself, just before drifting off to sleep. Tell your subconscious something like this: Tonight, I want you to give me only pleasant, safe, beautiful dreams, in which I shall be a hero, playing out a romantic life in which all my dreams shall come true.

When you have programmed your higher mind with that statement, go over some of the ugly, unhappy, and unfortunate experiences you have had in your past life. Start with your earliest memories and mentally review them in brief flashes, just as though you were watching them flash onto a motion picture screen. Many times you will find that these unfortunate and tragic mental images have been buried in your subconscious since your earliest childhood and must be aired to remove them fully.

Review your childhood frustrations, rages, and failures, and then correct them by telling yourself: I am now an adult; these childhood memories and experiences have no power over me and I now reprogram my higher mind with positive, happy, successful mental images that will remove all these painful thorns from my subconscious.

When you have carried out this dream catharsis of your own personal misfortunes and tragedies, go into the world scene and remove the historical incidents that you would like to be able to forget. Some of these may be: two or three wars that have occurred in the lifetimes of many people alive today; the Hitler episode, with the slaughter of 6 million people in gas chambers; the assassinations of the Kennedy brothers, Martin Luther King, and others that have left an ugly blotch on humanity's memory; the misery of fighting going on in Lebanon, Ireland, Africa, and other places; the ugly memories of Korea, Vietnam, and other such episodes that have taken an enormous toll of lives and left unhealthy mental images in millions of minds; the shame of political corruption in high places, such as the Watergate scandal in Nixon's presidency.

6. When you have mentally cleared your dream slate of all these ugly, painful pictures you are ready to reprogram your higher psychic mind centers with beautiful, inspiring, successful, and joyous experiences that you will now project to your dream world and make into living reality.

This conscious programming sets the stage for your dreams to be acted out realistically, and even prophetically, on the mental psychic screen of your higher intuitive mind.

Read this statement, or make up thoughts similar to these, and repeat them just before drifting off to sleep:

I now wish to program my subconscious with these new thought forms and mental images. I desire a clear mind, which shall do its work in an atmosphere of peace and tranquility.

I project the mental image of perfect health, mentally and physically.

I wish to be a loving person, attracting love and giving love.

I wish to function as an integrated human being, enjoying social reciprocity and working well with others.

I desire financial security and all that it implies in the way of leisure, culture, travel, and fulfillment of my dreams.

I wish to program a charming and magnetic personality so that I shall be attractive to others and be well liked.

I would like to remove from my higher psychic centers all feelings of guilt, inferiority, and self-consciousness.

I want to function perfectly in love relations with my true soul mate so that I can find fulfillment in love and marriage, bringing up my own family in a harmonious and joyful environment.

I want to have peace of mind and peace of soul so that I can fulfill my cosmic destiny on the mental, physical, and spiritual planes of expression.

WHY PROGRAMMING IS IMPORTANT

You may wonder why you have to program yourself with these perfect images in order to achieve psychic dreams that can guide you to the pattern of destiny you have chosen.

We now know scientifically that the subconscious can be conditioned to anything we choose. The Russian scientist Ivan Pavlov proved this. When he rang a bell, just before feeding his dogs, the dogs' salivary glands began secreting fluids in preparation for the food they were about to digest. Each time the bell rang before feeding, the same stomach and other bodily secretions began to flow. Later, when the bell was rung, but without the accompanying food, the dogs' glands secreted in exactly the same way.

These experiments led to the conditioned reflex theory, which we may also refer to as mental programming.

If your higher mind centers have been programmed with the alarm bells of fear, hate, worry, anxiety, war, disaster, sickness, accident, old age, poverty, insanity, and death—which is true for most people in this modern age—then you are causing your mental and bodily reactions to be patterned after these things, and you will constantly be under the whiplash of negative glandular chemistry preparing you for disaster.

On the other hand, if you have programmed yourself with the positive emotions of confidence, happiness, love, peace, joy, success, health, and youth, you will set the stage for these forces to be enacted in your dreams and projected to the outer world of reality.

REVIEW OF POINTS IN CHAPTER ONE

1. Most people dream one dream every ninety minutes of sleep, and these dreams are often prophetic and clairvoyant.
2. Jules Verne dreamed up 200 inventions that came true in our modern world.
3. A country girl dreamed herself into an operatic career at the Metropolitan Opera House in New York City.
4. Your dreams can be controlled and made to accurately predict your future so that the past, present, and future become one in the flow of the stream of consciousness.
5. You can use your dream consciousness to solve your problems, to act out a drama of comedy, tragedy, or romance on the stage of life.

6. You can create your own dream schedule, accurately projecting onto the psychic screen of your higher mind the events you want to occur in your life.

7. Robert H. dreamed that he had won a lot of money at the racetrack and played his dreamed-of numbers in the daily double at the Santa Anita Racetrack, winning $35,000.

8. You can create a mental psychic screen onto which you can project images of things you want to create and then dream these images to life.

9. A young lieutenant dreamed of his perfect soul mate, and he later met her, married her, and brought up a family, just as his dreams had prophesied.

10. You can sensitize your mental psychic screen to create any gifts or talents you desire.

11. You can give yourself a dream catharsis, to rid yourself of failure, fear, sickness, age, tragedy, death, and other negative forces.

12. You can use subconscious programming to project into your dream consciousness all the elements you want in your destiny.

13. Pavlov's conditioned reflex theory can work for you.

2
HOW TO USE YOUR DREAMS TO BUILD YOUR FUTURE DESTINY

Did you ever have a dream in which you were a famous person—like an opera star, a senator, or a well-known author? Such dreams represent your subconscious's projection of wish-fulfillment fantasies. Your secret and repressed longings to be famous, rich, and successful have gone underground in your mature years because others may have scoffed at these expressed desires.

In your dreams you may take on any personality you choose. You may choose any career you desire. You can take your place in the White House as president, with all the glory and none of the headaches that go with that high office. You can become as rich as Rockefeller or Getty without the burden of handling such a vast fortune. You can become Robert Redford or Elizabeth Taylor and never grow old or lose your popularity.

This is why dreams are so universal and popular; you can act out all your beautiful fantasies against any background you choose and be a character who is beautiful, popular, and beloved.

You may be mired down in a job you hate with a boss who is a Simon Legree, but in your dreams you can be the head of a vast organization with the power to hire and fire.

Your real life may be one of frustration in romance and misery in a marriage that has gone sour, but in your dreams you can be married to your soul mate and have a family that gives you no problems but great pleasure.

You have the power to select the dream fantasies you wish to live in while you sleep at night, and then when you awaken, to capture the memory of those ideal situations that your subconscious projected in your dreams.

The dream world represents a realm where all things are possible and where you can be an actor in any setting you choose. You can be a suave sophisticate in international society like a Jacqueline Kennedy Onassis or a Gore Vidal. You can be a comedian like Bob Hope, with the power to win the plaudits of kings and presidents, and you can own vast estates and castles in Spain without leaving the safe, comfortable domain of your own bed.

The fact of the matter is, as scientists are now proving in the laboratories in their study of dreamology, you have the power to project your desires and aspirations to your subconscious and it will work out the details of how you can achieve them, presenting them to you in vivid, realistic dreams. You must have the knowledge to interpret these dreams and then the courage to follow elusive will-o'-the-wisps to ultimate fulfillment.

This is what we shall now study: How to dream your desires into reality and make the dream come true.

REGIMEN FOR BUILDING YOUR DESTINY WITH YOUR DREAMS

1. Each night when you go to bed, prepare your subconscious with a series of vivid, visual images of some of the things you want your subconscious to incorporate in your dreams.

Select the type of person you wish to be and build this new self-image in your subconscious. You must project your choice to this higher subconscious, so it can get busy casting you in the roles you have selected for your life.

Are you a romantic lover whom others adore? If your dreams are filled with beautiful, idealistic actions that cause you to be happy and fulfilled, then you are already playing the role of the romantic lover. But if you have continual nightmares that your romance or marriage is ending in disaster or frequent dreams that you are searching for your true soul mate, the chances are that you are not playing the role of a romantic and successful lover in your everyday life of reality.

A Woman Acted Out Her Romantic Frustrations in Her Dreams

Teri J. came to me for counselling about her marital problems. She had been married for five years and had two lovely children, but lately she told me her husband had become cold and withdrawn, seldom desiring sexual intercourse. This frustration and the fear that she was losing him to another woman caused her to overeat, and she became so overweight that none of her clothes fit and she had to buy a complete new wardrobe.

Teri J. told me tearfully, "I don't know what's gone wrong in my life. I still love my husband, but everything I do seems to annoy him. Since the children came, he's been less attracted to me sexually, and when I began to put on weight, he told me that he has always hated fat women and found me most unattractive." As she dried her tears, she looked up at me with a pitiful expression on her face and asked, "Do you think it's possible for me ever to win my husband's love back?"

This was a simple question without a simple answer. I knew that something in Teri's psyche had been terribly upset, and so I asked her to tell me about her dreams, hoping that they would give me a clue as to what was wrong.

She said, "I hate to tell this dream, but I have it more and more lately. I seem to be a young, slender girl as I used to be, and I find myself in a bar, a kind of dive that I have never gone to in my life, but in my dream I find myself talking to men who admire me and want to go home with me. I seem to enjoy flirting with them and several times, in my dreams, I have actually gone to bed with different men and—" She hesitated a moment, as though acutely embarrassed at what she was going to say: "The awful thing about it is that I actually enjoyed going with those strange men, as if I were a—a prostitute!"

I hastened to assure Teri that there was nothing terrible about her dream; it was a mere reliving of a memory pattern buried deep in her subconscious of pleasure she had derived from the sexual act with her husband in years past. Then I assured her that many good, moral women, who would never think of being unfaithful to their husbands, dream of being prostitutes.

"What your dream is saying, Teri," I said, "is that you must go back and play the role of the lovely, slender young girl you once were, and you will once again have the admiration and love of your husband. Your subconscious is trying to tell you that you are still the same person you were before, when your husband loved you, and that to become that person again, you must lose weight, win back his love, and then safeguard it in the future."

I then gave Teri a personal plan that she would follow to make herself sexually and romantically attractive once more. She was put on a reducing program by her doctor, and I told her how to build the romantic self-image that would bring back the bloom of love in her marriage.

I am happy to say that this plan worked for Teri; she lost weight, she began to do little things that won back her husband's love. She rebuilt her self-image of romance, beauty, and charm so strongly that her husband again found her attractive, and to this day they are still happily married.

2. In selecting the character you wish to play in the drama of your own life, remember there are many different kinds of people who act out all kinds of roles, some good and some bad.

For instance, you may choose to play the part of a chronic complainer and faultfinder. Such persons are seldom attractive to others. Their lives are usually spent looking at the bad side of life and seldom seeing the good things that are all around them.

You may select the role of a loser and failure in your life drama. If this is your self-image, don't be surprised at the numerous failures and losses you have. If you are playing this role, your dreams will always be vague unsatisfied longings in which you are about to achieve some big goal when it vanishes and you never recapture it. Such dreams are usually cast against a backdrop of shabbiness, discomfort, and despair.

Dreams That Reveal Frustrations, Losses, and Failures

Typical dreams that signify life experiences of deprivation, losses, failures, and frustrations are of a person searching for something but unable to find it and awakening with a feeling of great loss, or a person dreams that he has just gotten a big job he really likes at a terrific salary when something goes wrong and he loses it.

Sometimes the dreamer casts himself in the role of a rich person who goes on a spending spree at Las Vegas or the race-track and finally loses his entire fortune. These dreams of losses and failure are always accompanied by feelings of deep depression when the dreamer awakens, for they are so realistic that they seem to be warnings to the dreamer of what he faces in the future. However, most people with failure syndromes do not recognize these warning dreams, and they continue playing the role of the failure and the misfit in their daily lives.

Do You Play a Tragedian's Role in Your Dreams?

There are many thousands of people who play the life role of a tragedian. These people seem to have tragedies and disasters that go way beyond the range of normality. They have cast themselves in these grim roles, and they seem to convert all of life's experiences into accidents, sickness, broken bones, and even premature death.

The dreams of such people are generally filled with tragedy. In their dreams they often project car accidents in which they are maimed or killed. They awake from these nightmares terrified and unable to go back to sleep. They sometimes dream that they are believed dead and placed in a coffin. In the dream, they awake and are suffocating. Then when they try to scream for help, they find that they are paralyzed and unable to make a sound. Such dreamers usually wake up with an indescribable feeling of terror.

A Girl Who Dreamed Herself into Tragedy

Joyce L., a girl of twenty-two, once came to me for advice on her problems. She was very attractive, and to look at her lovely face, with its beautiful expression, one would never dream of the tortured mind she possessed. With almost a smile she set to work to tell me of a series of tragedies and misfortunes that had followed her since her early childhood when she became an orphan. These unhappy events included a frightening episode of being molested as a child, which had caused her to fear and hate men.

Then she said, "I dream very often that I have committed suicide. I stand beside my coffin looking at myself and I seem to be dressed in white like a bride, and my face has such a happy expression on it that I feel no sadness when I awaken. I've had this dream many times recently and sometimes I wonder if it can be prophetic—perhaps it is trying to tell me that I should kill myself to end my suffering."

Then she proceeded to tell me, "You know I was born in the sign of Gemini, and I read somewhere Geminis often kill themselves. Marilyn Monroe was a Gemini, you know."

I stopped her from continuing this grim recital and hastened to say, "Yes, I know she was a Gemini, but all Geminis are *not* suicidal; look at Bob Hope, Henry Kissinger, Chad Everett, and the Duchess of Windsor—all born in Gemini and doing very well indeed." Then I explained to her that our dreams often reflect our life situations, and if we change these from tragedy and misfortune to lives of fulfillment and joy, our dreams automatically change.

I did not see this girl again, but a month later her aunt telephoned my office to say that Joyce had taken an overdose of sleeping pills and had indeed died a suicide.

Could this tragedy have been avoided? I believe that Joyce could have been helped with psychotherapy if she had wanted help. She could have changed the pattern of her dreams by changing the pattern of her life. I do not think in this case that her dreams were prophetic so much as that they reflected the conscious role of a tragedienne she had chosen to play in her life. If she had changed her self-image and made it one of beauty, romance, and happiness, her dreams would have reflected this state of consciousness and she would have had a life of fulfillment.

3. What is the ideal type of role that you can select for your life drama? Obviously, everyone wants to be a heroic figure. No one

wants to play the role of a villain, and yet, how many do enact just such a disagreeable role! They are the people who go through life with a chip on their shoulder; they are sarcastic, cynical, complaining, giving nothing to others in the way of smiles, kindness, or love.

Choose to be a hero and *not* a villain in your life drama. You will soon imprint your subconscious with this desire, and then see how amazingly your dreams reflect this change of mental attitude.

Program This New Self-Image in Your Dream Life

To program your dream consciousness with this new self-image of a hero, when you go to bed each night give yourself the following autosuggestions. You can memorize these to use or you can make up your own, but repeat the words to yourself just before drifting off to sleep, and then your subconscious will set to work to make them a reality for you.

I now program my subconscious with the following suggestions: I wish to have the rich rewards in life that come to those who are positive, confident, and have an awareness of their true worth. I wish to play the role of a romantic lover, to be attractive to others, to be sought after, admired, and respected. I choose to become idealistic and to be worthy of the best that life has to offer.

When you have programmed your subconscious for a period of two or three weeks with this idealistic statement of your role in life, you will change the very nature of your dreams. You will begin to see yourself successful, having experiences that are so pleasant that when you awake from your dreams you will want to go back to sleep to finish them!

4. You can flash onto the psychic screen of your higher mind the pictures that you wish to incorporate in your psyche so that they can be projected to the outer, objective world in actions that lead to the fulfillment of your desires.

This can be done at night, after you have said your autosuggestions to program your subconscious. As explained in chapter 1, you can mentally see a screen across your inner forehead onto which you will project the pictures, or thought forms, of the things you want to happen in your life.

When this is done as a conscious act, it is called daydreaming. Daydreams have created much that is enduring and worthwhile. The airplane was daydreamed into existence by Leonardo da Vinci who drew the first sketch of a plane without a motor. When he built it, the glorified glider flew a few feet off a roof and then crashed. However, under the original sketch of his magnificent dream, Leonardo wrote, "Man shall one day grow wings."

You can incorporate your wildest daydreams into these psychic flashes that you project onto your mental screen. You need not worry about whether they will come true or not; you merely project them and then let your subconscious catch them up and release them in vivid dreams while you sleep.

How to Project Psychic Pictures of Money in Your Dreams

Here are some psychic pictures you may project, with their possible corresponding dream patterns.

Picture yourself winning a lottery for $100,000 or more. Visualize what fun it would be to go on a shopping spree and buy anything you desire. You can daydream yourself into Las Vegas or the racetrack and see yourself winning large sums of money. As you project these vivid pictures on your psychic screen, go through the emotions of winning and feel the joy, the satisfaction, that comes from being financially secure.

These daydreams of financial security may also include getting the perfect job, owning your own business, or investing in the stock market, real estate, or commodities and making a fortune.

When these desires are converted into dream patterns you are apt to have any of the following dreams. See if any of these fit your own dreams.

You dream you find money on the street and pick up large bills. You marvel that no one else has discovered them. You may dream that you have just been left a million dollars by some distant relative. You may also dream that you are moving into a mansion with beautiful furnshings, and that you have an expensive car with a chauffeur at the wheel and are being admired by all your friends.

Your dreams may begin to take shape in patterns of great success in some business venture where you have a large staff working for you, and you are buying and selling some product that is making you a millionaire.

Many people believe that to dream of money means you will lose money, but it is actually an indication from your subconscious that you are very concerned about increasing your income or making a fortune.

If you persistently dream of losing money, this could represent subconscious anxiety about your bills and your inability to pay them. Or it could be a subconscious warning to get out of the job you are in (the losing process) and move up into a more worthy position that will increase your income.

OTHER DREAMS THAT SIGNIFY INCREASES IN INCOME

1. You may dream of looking at beautiful diamonds or other jewels with the intention of purchasing them for yourself or a beloved.
2. You may see yourself on a world cruise ship associating with wealthy people and visiting foreign lands.
3. If you dream several times that you have written a song that has made you a million dollars, this could be a subconscious nudge to examine your creative talents. Such a dream may also clothe itself in other creative acts, such as writing a novel and winning public acclaim; inventing something that makes a million dollars for you; becoming a famous opera star, actor, director, or producer in TV or motion pictures. Such creative dreams usually signify that your subconscious is ready to give you the knowledge and information you may require to achieve the high goals shown in your dream.

A Georgia Chain Gang Prisoner Dreamed Himself into Success

An example of how these dreams are often prophetic is that of a man who was a prisoner in a Georgia chain gang. His future seemed clouded and uncertain, but he had developed the habit of daydreaming while he worked, with the cruel chains biting into his ankles. He kept projecting mental pictures that he would one day be able to rise above his misfortunes and become famous.

In his dreams at night, he saw himself writing a famous novel that would be made into a motion picture and for which he would receive $100,000.

These dreams kept his hopes alive, until the day he was finally released from prison, when he headed towards New York City to begin the strangest adventure of his life.

His subconscious had been so programmed by his dreams of writing a great novel that he found himself automatically driven to buying a typewriter and sitting down before a blank page each day to write. Oddly enough, he had been so programmed to this creative idea that the thoughts and words poured forth, even though he had never before written a novel.

The results of all this activity were amazing; he found an agent who got a publisher for the novel. Though it was not a great success, selling only about one thousand copies, a motion picture company bought the movie rights to the book for $100,000, just the amount the ex-prisoner had been projecting in his dreams of success. He was taken to Hollywood to write the script, and you may have seen it on the screen with Paul Newman playing the title role in *Cool Hand Luke*. Dreams do have a way of coming true!

So project these dreams of your success and fortune every night onto your psychic screen and let them be clothed in the substance of reality.

REVIEW OF POINTS IN CHAPTER TWO

1. You can dream yourself into being an opera star, a senator, a well-known author, or anyone else you choose, and mentally project this dream to make it your destiny.

2. The world of fantasy, which includes your desires and aspirations, can be converted into the substance of realistic, vivid dreams.

3. Choose the self-image you wish to project to your subconscious, so that you cast yourself in a romantic, idealistic, and prosperous role in your life.

4. Teri J. acted out her frustrations of lost love, and in her dreams became an ignoble person. Through psychotherapy she learned what her dreams really meant.

5. You may play the role of a loser or winner, a happy or miserable person. Your dreams may show vague, unsatisfied yearnings and longings that are never satisfied.

6. Some typical dreams signify life experiences of deprivation, losses, frustrations, and failures.

7. Do you choose to play the role of a tragedian in life? Your dreams may then be of grim and tragic events.

8. Joyce L. dreamed herself into a tragedy and finally committed suicide because she did not know how to choose a less tragic role for her life drama.

9. You can have heroic dreams that show you winning in the game of life. Choose a good role, and your life will reflect fulfillment.

10. You can program your subconscious with autosuggestions to be rich, positive, romantic, attractive, and worthy of the best life has to offer.

11. You can learn how to use the psychic screen of your higher mind to project subjective dream patterns of health, happiness, and success.

12. Daydreams are important for creating subconscious patterns of success and fulfillment in life. For example, Leonardo da Vinci daydreamed the first airplane into existence.

13. Typical psychic pictures that you can project of yourself include winning $100,000 or more, finding money on the street, writing a novel, or being left a million dollars.

14. A prisoner on a Georgia chain gang dreamed himself into writing a novel, which was made into a motion picture for which he received $100,000.

3

THE UNIVERSAL SYMBOLOGY OF DREAMS AND HOW TO USE IT FOR YOUR BENEFIT

There are certain dreams that speak in a universal language that the average person can easily interpret. In order to use these symbols to predict your future, you should know a few things about the symbology of dreams.

First, do not accept the idea that all dreams must be interpreted as having sexual significance. Freud, in his earlier studies, believed that most dreams were sex-related. However, modern researchers in dreamology have found that the subconscious uses dreams to translate life experiences into messages to the dreamer. For example, if a person's life is filled with boredom, hard work, and poverty, he may dream of yachts, country clubs, high society, and million-dollar transactions in the stock market. This does not mean that the person's subconscious is trying to deceive him, but it is simply sending him a message that says in effect, "Look, this life you're living is a bore; get out of your work, your environment, and choose something more beautiful, glamorous, and successful."

In a leading research study of 10,000 dreams it was found that a person seldom dreams about his routine work or humdrum daily activities but generally takes on a new identity, a new life, and an environment quite different from his everyday one. This proves that the subconscious does not want to dwell in the restricted activities of the job, the small income, and the shabby environment the dreamer lives in but prefers to paint a picture of the life that could be if the dreamer would awaken to his potential for greatness.

We shall now learn what this universal symbology of your dreams is trying to show you in picture form, which we call dreams. Then you can interpret your own future dreams and use them as psychic guidelines to future courses of action that will bring you fulfillment of your dreams.

Some of the common symbols that appear most frequently in dreams are the following:

DREAMS OF FALLING THROUGH THE AIR

This dream could be interpreted in several ways; it may be presenting a psychic picture of a future downfall that awaits the dreamer when he is flying high or being very successful. It often represents the subconscious's belief that some catastrophe awaits the individual, and it is warning him to prepare for it.

A man who had invested heavily in the stock market often had the dream that he was flying, and he experienced an exhilarating sensation while he soared like a bird high above the earth. The thing that he didn't like, however, was when he discovered that he did not really have wings and, in sudden fear, began to fall to earth. He would awake from these dreams in anxiety, wondering what they could possibly mean.

A few months later the stock market, in which he had invested most of his savings, suddenly collapsed, sending his stocks plummeting and losing him most of his fortune. Had this man been aware of the psychic content of his flying dreams, he might have taken steps to avert the disaster.

The subconscious often takes stock of a situation in real life and apprehends the hidden dangers or threats that exist there, presenting its findings in the form of dreams. If you are clever enough to search your dreams for their objective content and then analyze them in reference to your own particular life situation, you may have an accurate gauge of events that are foreshadowed in your future and you may be able to take steps to avoid those that bring disasters, accidents, and losses.

DREAMS OF FLYING ABOVE THE EARTH

A dream that one is flying, without the sudden falling, could symbolize the fact that your life lacks inspiration and has fallen into a pattern of dullness, mediocrity, and boredom. You long to escape your work, your home problems, your debts and worries; since you cannot physically escape, your subconscious takes you into fanciful flights above the earth where you are temporarily free of your burdens.

Such dreams of flying that bring exhilaration and joy can be interpreted as your subconscious desire to free yourself of a job that bores you, or it could indicate the higher aspirations of your psychic mind, which is trying to tell you that you can rise above your limitations and soar into the boundless realms of success, riches, fame, and prosperity.

If you accept this interpretation of your flying dream, you will take steps to improve your mind and seek out a better situation in life. You will examine your own work, your home life, your social activities with a critical mind, trying to find ways in which you can improve yourself and reach the high goals that your subconscious is trying to point out.

Robert R. Dreamed His Way to a $5,000 Bonus

Robert R., who worked in an advertising agency, had such high-flying dreams. He told me when he came for consultation that he soared like a bird and enjoyed his flying sessions but awakened a little disappointed that he could not fly as he did in his dreams. He said, "In my dreams, when I am flying, I can see people's upturned faces on earth, staring at me in amazement and admiration. But when I wake up and find myself like any ordinary mortal, I always feel very let-down and depressed."

In analyzing his dream, I explained to this young man that he was probably bored with his nine-to-five job and longed to be free of the pressures and responsibilities of his life. He admitted that he was constantly worried, as he had bought a new home, had a wife and child to support, and his money scarcely stretched far enough to meet his heavy obligations. This was the clue to the meaning of his flying dreams—a desire to get away from it all.

I then told him that his subconscious was trying to project a dream of the future that could be his. "Why don't you try to free yourself of the limitations of your job and seek out some new endeavor that will give you a chance to soar to new levels of successful achievement."

A few weeks later Robert came to me beaming with joy. He had had another dream in which he saw an idea for advertising a product of a client company and he had gone to the head of the agency with the idea. When it was presented to the company, which happened to be a big drug corporation, they were so delighted with it that a campaign was started to promote the idea on TV and in newspapers and magazines throughout the country. Robert was given a bonus of $5,000, and he started on the road to even greater success.

Later, inspired by his flying dreams, he was able to open his own advertising agency, where he became more successful than he had ever dreamed possible.

DREAMS OF FINDING MONEY ON THE STREET OR IN STRANGE PLACES

This common type of dream often occurs with people who are not aware that the subconscious is trying to lead them to finding new ways of making money. Very often they will dream of finding money on the street and picking up large bills, worried that someone is watching. At other times the money may be concealed in an unusual place, like the secret compartment of a bureau drawer or an attic.

A Young Woman Dreamed of Money Hidden in a Secret Drawer

A young woman who had nursed her father through a long and costly illness finally lost him in death. Her mother was already dead, and after her father's funeral expenses were paid, the girl found herself broke, unable to get a job and with no one to help her.

One night she had a vivid dream in which her father came to her. He looked exactly as he had in life, and his voice was the same as she remembered it. Her father looked very anxious and concerned as he said, "I know how worried you are about money, but I did not leave you without providing for your future. Look in the antique chest of drawers in the living room. You will find a secret compartment back of the first drawer where I had put away money for your future."

When the girl awakened, she could still hear her father's voice ringing in her ears. She got up, turned on the light, and went to the living room, where she opened the drawer. There, in a secret compartment, just as her father had revealed in the dream, was a large roll of $100 bills, totaling $15,000!

DREAMS OF SOME FEROCIOUS ANIMAL ABOUT TO DEVOUR ONE

This type of dream occurs frequently to people who have deep anxieties and fears about the future. It sometimes is a psychic dream that warns of impending disaster. Often it is used by the subconscious as a symbol to warn of illness (a devouring of the physical body) or calamities that threaten the physical self, a business, or a marriage.

Her Husband's Affair with Another Woman Revealed in a Dream

A woman had this type of recurring dream: a tiger was in hot pursuit, just about to pounce on her. As she fled she turned to look back at her pursuer. The tiger had the face of a beautiful blond woman!

A few weeks later this woman happened to pass by a restaurant where her husband often had lunch. She looked in the window and saw her husband in a booth with a beautiful blond woman! Later she found out that her husband was having an affair with this woman, and she then realized why she had had the prophetic dream of a tiger about to devour her. Fortunately, she told me, she and her husband were able to patch things up and remain together for the sake of their two young children.

Warnings of Disease through Dreams of Ferocious Animals

To dream of danger through any kind of animal could be a signal from your subconscious that there is some physical ailment that may not yet have surfaced. A woman dreamed that a ferocious dog, like a Great Dane, was standing over her chest about to devour her bare breasts. She awakened in terror with a feeling of great anxiety. Two weeks later, examining her breasts, she found an incipient tumor. When it was removed, it was found to be malignant. The subconscious often masks in universal symbols things the conscious mind hates to face. The cancer that literally "devours" the body cells is disguised in a dream as a ferocious animal about to devour one.

DREAMS OF A COFFIN, DEATH, OR BEING BURIED ALIVE

This common type of dream often symbolizes the dreamer's subconscious fear of death and disintegration. But sometimes it means the dying of a romance or a business or the passing of an era. Generally, people who have this type of dream fear death, and they especially fear being buried alive.

She Dreamed She Was Being Buried Alive

One woman had the recurring dream of being locked in a coffin and trying to scream out, "I'm alive! I'm alive! Don't bury me!" She would awake from these dreams in a cold sweat, not wanting to go back to sleep for fear the same dream would haunt her. When she came to me for consultation, I discovered that she had only begun to have this dream two years before, when she found out that her marriage was on the rocks. Her religion prohibited her from getting a divorce, so she had been figuratively locked into a situation that was a "living death." When this was pointed out to her and she underwent psychotherapy to help her face her problem consciously and do something constructive about it, the troublesome dreams stopped.

Presidents Who Have Dreamed of Assassination

The dream of death is often prophetic; the subconscious apprehends some danger signal and tries to communicate this warning through a dream.

Abraham Lincoln had such a prophetic dream. He told the members of his household that he had had a disturbing dream. He saw people all around him crying and asked them, "Why do you weep?" They replied, "A president has died."

He said he walked into the Blue Room in the White House, where he saw a flag-draped coffin. He went close and looked inside. There he saw his own face staring up at him! One week later this dream sequence became a living reality. Had Lincoln obeyed his warning psychic dream, he might have lived.

A similar story is told about John F. Kennedy. A few days before his trip to Dallas, he told members of his family that he had a dream in which he saw an assassin firing at him. He was begged to cancel his trip, but he laughed off the incident as being only a dream. The course of history might have been changed if he had obeyed his higher psychic mind, which was trying to warn him of impending disaster!

DREAMS OF SNAKES, CRAWLING INSECTS, OR LICE COULD SYMBOLIZE SEVERAL DIFFERENT THINGS

A Freudian psychiatrist might ascribe dreams of snakes to the phallic symbol of a penis or make other interpretations involving sex in various forms. But Freud's colleague Carl Gustav Jung was not convinced that all dreams had their bases in sexual experiences. He believed that the subconscious often disguised in dreams things that the dreamer could not consciously face without experiencing psychic pain. A dream of snakes might thus imply that one has fears that pertain to his security or well-being.

A Society Woman Had Dreams of Being Covered with Lice

A society woman often had a dream in which she was beautifully dressed, wearing expensive jewelry, and being admired by her guests, when she suddenly realized that she was covered with lice! Seeing these creatures, her guests turned and fled.

When I talked to this woman about her life experiences, I found out that she came from a southern family that had lost all their money. She hated her father because he had dissipated their fortune, and she had made up her mind she would one day marry a man of wealth and become a social leader.

Driven by this obsession, she did marry a wealthy lawyer, and they became outstanding social leaders in their community, but always underlying her success was the fear that she would one day be found out and lose her hard-won social gains.

When this was pointed out to the woman, she saw immediately that the lice were projections of her subconscious fears, and she was able to rid herself of this obsession and go on to even greater enjoyment of her social life.

Snakes in a Dream as Warnings of Illness or Anxiety

A dream of being bitten by a snake could be a warning from the subconscious that some business or social contact might bring about harm or danger. A dream of walking into a room filled with crawling snakes could signify that one is in a situation that might prove troublesome or dangerous. Threats against one's security, anxiety about illness, or family problems could cause such dreams of snakes or other animals or insects that threaten one's safety.

Later, we shall explore many other universal symbols that can give you clues as to what your dreams are trying to tell you, and show how you can use this knowledge to accurately predict events in your own future.

REVIEW OF POINTS IN CHAPTER THREE

1. Dreams often mask themselves in universal symbols that are trying to give psychic warnings of events about to occur.
2. The old Freudian idea that all dream symbols relate to sex is erroneous; modern researchers find that these symbols often stand for things other than sex.
3. A study by a leading researcher of 10,000 dreams reveals that most dreamers take on new identity or project themselves into lives of adventure, excitement, and romance to make up for the humdrum nature of their own lives.
4. The dream of flying through the air and landing suddenly is often a psychic warning that there will be a sudden collapse of a business, a marriage, or some other project.
5. Sometimes such a dream signifies a desire to climb up the ladder of success and achieve high financial or social goals.
6. A man who had a dream of flying and then crashing had all his money in the stock market when it suddenly collapsed and lost him his fortune.
7. A young man in an advertising agency dreamed of flying; he later dreamed up a new idea for his firm that won him a $5,000 bonus.
8. The dream of finding money on the street or in strange places often symbolizes the opportunity for new investments or finding a new source of income.
9. A young woman had a dream of finding money, and she later discovered $15,000 hidden in a secret compartment of an antique dresser.
10. A dream of a ferocious animal about to pounce can be a symbol of some physical ailment that the subconscious is trying to warn of, or it may indicate fears and anxieties about the future.
11. A woman who dreamed that a Great Dane dog was about to devour her breasts awakened in terror. Later examination showed she had a malignant tumor in a breast. She was saved by treatment.
12. A woman dreamed of being chased by a tiger with the face of a beautiful blond woman. Later she found out her husband was having an affair with a beautiful blond woman.

13. Dreams of death or of being locked in a coffin while still alive can be prophetic, or they can symbolize being locked into a job, a marriage, or any other life situation that is figuratively "the kiss of death."

14. Abraham Lincoln and John F. Kennedy had dreams of assassination, which could have helped them to avoid death if they had obeyed these psychic warnings.

15. The dream of snakes or crawling insects, lice, or other things crawling on the body could symbolize fear of exposure or fear of threats to security, romance, or position in life.

16. A society woman dreamed that lice were all over her and that her guests saw them and fled. She feared exposure of her lowly background.

4
HOW TO RECEIVE INSTRUCTIONS FOR CREATIVE EXPRESSION FROM YOUR DREAMS

In life there are many round pegs in square holes, and vice versa, because people fail to follow their own intuitive and psychic impulses as to the creative work they could pursue.

How many times is a person told by his relatives, "You can't become an artist because you're completely untalented" or, "It's silly to try and become a singer; the world is overrun with them and besides, you don't have the voice"!

How many would-be authors, designers, composers, inventors, and actors have been thwarted by such well-meaning but shortsighted people who measure a person's talents and limitations by their own failings!

You can harness the power of your dreams so that you may receive instructions for any creative gifts you wish to develop. There is a saying that one learns how to ski in the summer. It is during this period, after the failures and frustrations on the ski slopes in winter, that the subconscious has an opportunity to examine the reasons for past failures and to devise new techniques to cope with inadequacies and problems. The same principle might apply to learning how to swim in the winter, when we can relive the efforts of the summer months and acquire greater proficiency in that sport.

So, too, you may acquire any great creative gift during the

hours spent in sleeping and dreaming once you learn how to program your subconscious with the right creative instructions.

A Young Woman Learned French in Her Dream World

A young woman wanted to get a job in the United States embassy in Paris, where she could meet interesting people and expand her cultural horizons. However, she did not speak French and this was necessary for such a job.

She asked my advice as to how she could achieve proficiency in this language in a few months' time. I told her to program her higher psychic mind with the desire to speak French. She was to have French lessons recorded on a tape recorder, which she would play for an hour before she went to sleep, giving the day's lesson to the subconscious. Then after a few such sessions, during the night, she would have the experience of dreaming she was speaking fluently in French.

At first she found herself floundering in her dreams, as her subconscious had not been fully saturated with the language. But in a few days, she was dreaming that she had the embassy job and was able to handle everyday French adequately for her position. These dreams became more and more vivid as time went on, and after four months, she was fluent enough in the language to apply for the job. She got it and found her dream fulfilled; she was living in Paris and enjoying a new life experience.

For this system, I drew on my own experience in learning to speak Greek when I visited that country for the first time some years ago. I was to stay there one year and I knew that it would be important to speak the language. I recorded Greek lessons on tape and played them over and over, especially at night before retiring. My subconscious absorbed the language as a child learns to speak, quite naturally and without great effort. Within six months I was dreaming in Greek and speaking the language quite well, although it is one of the most difficult of all languages to learn. I even dreamed that I was being interviewed on television in Athens and answering questions quite fluently in Greek, to the amazement of all concerned. A few weeks later, I met a television interviewer at the Hilton Hotel in Athens and she asked me if I would appear on a TV show and be interviewed in Greek!

REGIMEN TO PROGRAM YOUR SUBCONSCIOUS FOR CREATIVE GIFTS

1. First make up your mind what kind of creative expression you desire. If it is to become a composer, know whether you want to become a modern composer who caters to rock and roll enthusiasts or a classical composer like Chopin, Mozart, or Beethoven.
2. Now that you know what kind of composer you wish to be, program your subconscious with the type of music you want to compose. There are plenty of examples on recordings, on television, on radio, and in concert halls. Play this type of music over and over until you are literally saturated with the sounds of the music you wish to compose. This can be anything from hillbilly music, to spirituals, or even operatic music. Tell your higher psychic mind just before you go to sleep, "I want you to incorporate into my dreams the type of music I wish to compose. Show me how to be a composer. I want to give enjoyment to the world and also make money through my music."

Then in your dreams you will probably find yourself at the piano, composing brilliant songs, with the words already written for you. Often you will dream that you are performing your own compositions before vast audiences in a concert hall. You will no doubt receive a standing ovation for your performance! You can be anything you dream of being if you only long for it with enough enthusiasm and desire.

A Dream Placed a Cowboy Singer on the Stage of Carnegie Hall

An experience from my Carnegie Hall days, when I lectured to thousands of people every Sunday at 5:30 P.M., will show the potent power of dream fantasies to bring fulfillment of a person's dream. A young cowboy singer once appeared for an audition that I was giving to discover new singers for our Sunday programs. Naturally we only presented the finest trained voices, doing semiclassical and classical works. But this young man told me a story before his audition. He said, "My father was once an usher in Carnegie Hall in his younger days, when he wanted to become a famous singer and give a concert in that hall. He wasn't able to get the musical education he needed during the depression years, so he returned to Texas, married, and settled down. But over the years he kept having this dream of appearing before huge audiences in Carnegie Hall and making it big as a singer. When I was born, this same obsession was carried over into my life. He gave me piano and guitar lessons and told me about his youthful dream, only now he transferred it to me, saying, 'Son, one day you will have a chance to sing in Carnegie Hall, you just wait and see!'"

Well, I was deeply touched by the youth's story, and after hearing him sing, I realized that his voice would never make the Metropolitan Opera House, but he had an appealing Western style of singing that I knew audiences would respond to.

I wound up presenting this young man as a solo artist, introducing him as a singer of songs from the Western plains. And just as his father had dreamed he received a tremendous ovation from the three thousand people who were there that day. That was the first time a Western, or cowboy, singer had ever appeared on the stage of Carnegie Hall!

3. If you dream of becoming a great artist, apply this same technique to painting, designing, or any other branch of art you wish to express. Saturate yourself with knowledge about art, study the lives of the great artists, from the masters like Leonardo da Vinci and Michelangelo to the modern artists. Choose the particular branch of art in which you wish to excel, and then set to work each night before you go to sleep to program your subconscious with the idea that you are going to become an artist and receive recognition as such.

You may already have had dreams that were trying to guide you to such artistic and creative expression if you knew how to interpret them correctly. Do you often dream of scenes from nature, such as magnificent paintings in vivid, shimmering colors?

Do you often dream that you are creating a masterpiece of art that the world acclaims? Sometimes these creative inspirations will come in dreams that show you walking through an art gallery, viewing the masterpieces of past geniuses, only instead of their names being on the canvasses, you are startled to find your own.

Your superior psychic mind has many ways of trying to gently nudge you into creative expression of your gifts and talents. You may not be consciously aware of them, but this superpower knows your potentials as well as your limitations and will seldom steer you in the wrong direction in the symbolism it uses to mask your dreams.

Picasso Dreamed up His Art Fantasies and Changed His Life

The great modern artist Pablo Picasso at one time was a very fine classical painter, doing easily recognized subjects far different from those that marked his later career when surrealistic and impressionistic influences gave his works an "other-world look" that made him one of history's highest priced artists. He told the story that during the early period when he painted prosaic-looking subjects, he had a vivid dream in which he was painting a nude figure when suddenly he had an impulse to splash brilliant colors on his canvas, making irregular patterns over the surface of the model's face and body in brilliant colors and designs that finally completely disguised the woman's figure, making her look like some distorted dream fantasy.

This dream, in different forms, kept recurring to the great artist until he was so haunted by these erratic dream figments that he found himself irresistibly composing and painting such a subject, in what was to become his first phase of expressive painting. He never returned to his former style, but he produced masterpieces that today are acclaimed throughout the world.

Salvador Dali's Dreams Placed His Work in the Metropolitan Museum of Art

I once met Salvador Dali at a party in Greenwich Village, and we talked about the subject of dreams. His paintings are highly surrealistic, giving the impression that he has visited other worlds. Dali told me that he used to have a frequent dream that one day he would paint a picture that would hang in the Metropolitan Museum of Art in New York City. He said it seemed unlikely at that time but from the inspiration he received from that psychic dream, he began work on a painting of Christ on the Cross, which now hangs in that famous art museum!

4. How can you tell what creative gifts you possess and what you should try to express in your efforts to achieve success as a creative artist?

If your dreams persistently follow a certain pattern, you can be sure that your higher psychic mind is trying to nudge you in the direction of fame and fortune through creative or artistic work.

Such symbolical dreams may frequently occur, showing you doing the creative things that your subconscious knows you are capable of doing. You may have a suppressed desire to become a great author. By great, I mean commercially great, like Harold Robbins or Jacqueline Susann. Forget the literary merits of their work. I'm sure they laughed all the way to the bank over the critics' evaluations.

Your dreams may encompass such themes as autograph parties in which you are signing your first book. Or you may find yourself in your dreams sitting before a typewriter as thousands of words of brilliant writing pour out onto the blank sheets of paper. When you awake, you feel you have created a great novel and wish you could recall all the brilliant things you said in it. Actually, this type of dream means that you have the capacity to write and your subconscious higher mind is trying to communicate this to you.

Sometimes the dream will portray the fruits of your creative labors, and show you living in a mansion, hobnobbing with the rich and famous or riding in a chauffeur-driven Rolls Royce.

Or you may dream that your novel has been made into a movie and you are attending the premiere, escorting some glamorous movie star, and being introduced to the audience as the author of the epic being shown on the screen.

Generally, such dreams of fame and fortune imply that you have the latent capacity to rise to great creative achievements.

Your subconscious cloaks your aspirations in symbolical form and releases them as dreams. If you are clever in interpreting them, you can play along with this psychic twin that knows all, sees all, and is all, and achieve the things being projected on your psychic screen.

Often our dreams are the precursors of future events that are being projected by the subconscious as a hint of our real capabilities. If we follow these psychic guidelines to fame and fortune, everything will fall into its right place without great effort or strain. If we resist the pull of fate in the direction of greatness, we suffer from frustration and wind up being failures and experiencing nervous exhaustion and other forms of psychosomatic illness.

A Dream Placed Ronald Reagan in the Governor's Mansion

At the time when I was known as the adviser to the movie stars I once interviewed a beginning actor at Warner Brothers Studios in Hollywood. This young man, in his early twenties, told me that during the depression years, when work was almost impossible to get, he had a very vivid dream that he was a famous Hollywood movie star. This dream recurred over a period of months. Finally, unable to obtain the money to pay for the train ride to the movie capital, he began to hitchhike his way to the city of dreams. He finally reached a place in Arizona where he found himself at the foot of a mountain range at sunset. An attendant at a nearby gas station informed him that the place was called Inspiration Mountain. He told the young would-be actor that many a miner had died trying to find gold in this mountain range.

As the young man watched the gold-and-crimson sunset, he vowed to himself that his Inspiration Mountain was to be Hollywood, where he would find his pot of gold at the end of the rainbow. With this thought in mind, he went to sleep, confident that one day he would become a famous movie star.

That young man's dream came true shortly thereafter. Ronald Reagan, for it was he who told me this true story, went on to become not too great an actor, but he won political office as governor of California, and he could well be on a pathway that leads to another kind of Inspiration Mountain—the White House in Washington, D.C.!

5. There are other symbols and psychic indications that could be trying to point out your own capacity for future fame, fortune, and fulfillment of your dreams. These could be masked as attempts to climb a high mountain whose peaks are hidden by cloud banks. On your upward climb, in your dreams, you may run into obstacles. The rope you are climbing with may break, threatening you with imminent destruction; or you may come across barriers that stop your upward climb, leading you to descend in frustration and rage; or you may be trying to go upstream in a river, where you row against the currents and no matter how hard you try, the boat seems to be drifting downstream again.

Dreams of Frustration Pointed His Way to Success

These dreams of frustration and inability to reach your goal are indicative of the problems you face that keep you from rising to the mountain peaks of success or swimming up the river to your desired goals of fame and fortune.

One young man who frequently dreamed that he was in a space ship, going to a distant planet whose identity he did not know, kept experiencing difficulties on the way. He had undoubtedly been influenced by such TV dramas as *Star Trek* or *Space: 1999,* portraying people working and living in such space ships. In his dream he was often attacked by enemy tribes in other space ships and always awoke in panic just as he was about to land on the beautiful planet.

When he told me his dreams, I recognized immediately that he was experiencing frustrations in some kind of career effort. He then confessed that he had wanted to become a television director and producer but obstacles were continually put in his way. We then worked out a schedule of subconscious programming he was to use just before going to sleep at night, and he finally overcame the problems and was selected to direct his first TV show. He is now working steadily with one of the big networks and is a big success.

HOW TO PROGRAM YOUR PSYCHIC CENTERS FOR CREATIVE GENIUS

1. Each night when you go to bed, do your psychic dream-programming. The mind that knows all is waiting eagerly for your cooperation. As there are two minds involved in this process, the conscious and the subconscious, I have named them the Mental Twins. One twin, your conscious mind, has already been programmed with all the negative, discouraging suggestions that have made you decide to give up trying to become a creative genius.

Negative Programming Can Wreck Your Dreams of Success

One mental twin, your subconscious, is naturally prejudiced for your success, as it is favorable towards the idea of life, health, and great achievements. It only exists when you thrive; it flourishes when you are happy and successful; it basks in your glory and fame. This natural, God-given right to be healthy, happy, and successful is born in every infant. A child will have confidence that he can do anything he wants to do unless he is discouraged by parents or others. Do not tell him such things as: "You can't be a success"; "The rich have all the money, so forget about becoming rich"; "You were born on the other side of the tracks, so you will have to be unknown all your life"; "You're the wrong race, color, or creed, so you'll be discriminated against and can't expect to get to the top."

A Great Scientist Was Inspired to His Career by Dreams

I recall a meeting I once had with the noted black educator and horticulturist, George Washington Carver, at Tuskeegee Institute, in Alabama. He was born to parents who were slaves, and as a young man he had to face every known prejudice against his race. But he told me that in those early years of struggle he had vivid dreams that he would one day help liberate black people from prejudice and intolerance. He so programmed his subconscious in those years that he became one of the most outstanding agriculturists of his time. He discovered hundreds of products that could be made from peanuts, including wallboard, insulating materials, cattle feed, paints, and varnishes. He changed the economy of the South with his dreams.

2. To program your subconscious and prepare it for its great adventure in releasing inspiration that can make you a creative genius, start out by writing down some of the things you want your spiritual and psychic twin to do for you. It might look something like this:

(a) I wish to become a creative genius in something that I can do and that will bring me fame and fortune. Guide me in the direction of my greatest talents and show me the methods for achieving my high goals in life.

(b) I desire a home of my own. (Here simply describe the type of home you want.)

(c) I wish to be in my own business. (Here you can tell your psychic twin what kind of business you prefer. Be specific; if it is to be a restaurant owner, beautician, or caterer for parties, explain this in detail.)

(d) I wish to make the sum of $50,000 (or more) a year in my own business.

(e) I wish to be promoted in my work, with a raise in salary. (You may not want millions or a business of your own, but if you desire a raise in salary or a promotion, put this down so that your psychic twin can get busy showing you how to achieve this.)

(f) I want to find my true soul mate so that I may have happiness in love and marriage.

(g) I want a new car. (Here write down the make, model, and even the color of the car you want to own. Don't worry about where the money will come from to buy it; just put it down and let your psychic twin worry about how it's going to come.)

There is tremendous power in suggestions to your psychic mind, and when your psychic twin is ready to push you in the direction of your fame and fortune, it will reveal this in a pattern of dreams and symbols that will give clues as to how you are to achieve your future greatness.

Geniuses of History Were Created through Dream Power

Leonardo da Vinci, without knowing anything about his psychic twin, automatically used this method of psychic programming when he was only twelve years old. He was born out of wedlock, and in the Italy of that day he was a social outcast with little hope of ever rising to any degree of prominence. However the young Leonardo wrote in his diary, "I shall one day become a great artist and win world acclaim. I shall walk with kings and princes and live in palaces."

The great artist Joseph Turner had vivid dreams that inspired him to paint his magnificent seascapes. He had been to Venice as a young man and he never forgot the magnificent sunsets and sunrises over the canals. Years later he dreamed these scenes back into reality on his canvasses, which captured all the splendor of the beautiful scenes he had witnessed.

The story is told that when Turner showed his paintings in his London home, the visitor would be ushered into a darkened living room to wait a few moments before being admitted into the room where the paintings were beautifully lighted and exhibited. One guest asked Turner the purpose of this wait and the artist replied, "You must empty your eyes of the common glare before you are ready to see the purity and magnificence of my colors."

So, too, when you program your higher psychic dream-self with your new destiny, you should first empty your consciousness of all your old, preconceived ideas of poverty, lack, and limitation, or any other negative thoughts about your future or your abilities.

REVIEW OF POINTS IN CHAPTER FOUR

1. Many would-be authors, singers, actors, and composers are thwarted in achieving their dreams by relatives who program them with failure thoughts of poverty, lack, and limitation.

2. Dreams can give us clues as to our creative gifts and reveal methods for achieving the fulfillment of our aspirations.

3. A young woman used subconscious imprinting to learn French so that she could fulfill her desire to work in an American embassy in Paris, France.

4. You can program your subconscious, using dreamology to imprint your psychic mind with the methods for achieving the things you desire.

5. A Texas cowboy was guided by his father's dreams to an unprecedented appearance in world-famous Carnegie Hall.

6. If you wish to become a composer, author, or artist, or do any other highly creative work, train your higher mind to reveal the gifts and methods through your dreams.

7. Picasso used dream fantasies to begin his great career when he broke from traditional painting to impressionism.

8. Salvador Dali dreamed that he was being exhibited in the Metropolitan Museum of Art and was inspired to paint a great canvas that now hangs in that museum.

9. Your subconscious masks your ambitions and talents in universal symbols that can reveal the genius that lies within your own mind.

10. Dreams of living in a mansion, riding in an expensive automobile, or attending glamorous premieres or parties could be trying to nudge you in the direction of fame and fortune as a creative artist.

11. Ronald Reagan started on a career that may eventually lead him to the White House through a psychic dream that told him to go to Hollywood.

12. Often your dreams show frustrations, for example, climbing a mountain and being obstructed on the way or trying to row a boat upstream; these are all indications that you must work harder to achieve success.

13. One young man used his frustrating dreams of flying in a space ship to guide him to success as a TV director and producer.

14. You can discover and use your psychic twin to guide you to your own unfolding of genius within your higher psychic mind.

15. The noted black educator George Washington Carver used his dreams to guide him to the achievement of greatness in his work.

16. You can create your own psychic "blueprint of destiny" that can lead you to fulfillment of your every dream in life.

17. The great artist Leonardo da Vinci had psychic dreams that he would walk with kings, and live in palaces; his dreams came true.

5

"COMING EVENTS CAST THEIR SHADOWS BEFORE!" HOW YOUR DREAMS CREATE YOUR FUTURE

Everyone is influenced to a great extent by his dreams. Our fears and anxieties are often reflected in our dreams, shaping our actions to avoid the catastrophies that these dreams foretell. Our hopes and aspirations are often couched in the universal language of our dreams, foretelling the glories we shall experience, the fame we should strive to achieve, and the fortune that can be ours through releasing our higher, creative talents in our work.

THE TAPESTRY OF DREAMS THAT CREATES YOUR DESTINY

You can train your higher psychic twin, which rules over your dream world, to bring you the prophetic type of dream that reveals the fabric of your future destiny. In this tapestry of dreams, which becomes your destiny, you will find revealed the gold and silver threads of personal fame and fortune; the rose-colored threads of perfect romance with your true soul mate; the azure blue and sunlight gold of happiness, peace of mind, and inner tranquility. Here, too, sometimes there are revealed the somber threads of personal grief and tragedy: the loss of a loved one in death; the accidents, operations, illnesses, and bereavements that often cloud the horizons of our futures.

These dreams that masquerade in strange guises often mislead us, because we are not used to the psychic language of our dream world. Nothing here is as it seems; we may dream of clouds and rainstorms and believe that they portend disastrous events, such as losses of money, homes, or jobs, whereas in reality the psychic twin that controls dreams may be trying to forecast for you a period of prosperity and financial growth. Rain makes the earth spring into bloom, and often this type of dream is saying, "Plant the seedlings of reality in your garden of destiny, and they shall bloom in the springtime of your life with every good thing that you desire."

Similarly, you may dream of a funeral of someone precious to you. The symbolical language of your dreams may be trying to tell you to bury your fears and anxieties and release yourself of the burdens that hound you every day. You may be in a job that bores you; your social life may have become stale and unrewarding; your marriage that may have been made in heaven has become mired down after years of problems, poverty, or boredom. What your dreams are trying to tell you is, "Forget the past, bury your worries and your boredom, and face the resurrection of your hopes and dreams for a more brilliant future." Your own higher, psychic mind must tell you just what your dreams intend to convey to your conscious mind.

How a Man Became a Famous Explorer Because of His Dreams

Many years ago when I was lecturing at Carnegie Hall, I met a man who came to me for a consultation. He had bogged down in his career, was uncertain of the future, and wanted my advice as to how he could break the chain of misfortune and frustration that seemed to bind him.

At our first interview, he told me an oft-recurring dream that puzzled him. He said, "In this dream I find myself traveling through the jungles and plains of Africa and having all kinds of strange adventures. Wild animals are all around me, but I never seem to shoot them; I seem to be armed, not with a gun but with a movie camera. I can assure you this dream puzzles me. I have never had a desire to go to Africa, and as to photography, I wouldn't know which end of a movie camera to point at the subject. But I have a deep feeling that this dream is trying to reveal something to me that can help me in the future."

I told Lewis Cotlow, who is now a famous author, explorer, movie producer, and lecture personality, that his dream was indeed trying to tell him something. It was revealing to him what he already knew—that he was finished with his present career and was about to embark on a new adventure, possibly traveling to foreign countries, filming documentaries, and writing books about his exploits.

I told him, "You yourself may not know these facts consciously, because you have been so used to the routine of your everyday life, your present work, and living conditions that your psyche is programmed to your present activities. But if you listen to your psychic dreams, you will soon be prodded in the direction they are trying to point to."

I lost sight of Lewis Cotlow for two years, but when I next saw him, he was a changed person—buoyant, confident, and looking ten years younger. "You'll never guess what happened after that interview with you," he said. "I began to get interested in exploration; I even began to study cameras and methods of photographing wildlife, and I soon found myself with the money to finance a trip to Africa. I have just sold my first motion picture to one of the big Hollywood studios and it is being released this week in theaters throughout the country!" Cotlow made several other famous films showing his explorations of Africa and South America. He was the first person ever to photograph the Pygmy tribes who live deep in the African jungle and to bring back movies of the South American aborigines who are feared as headhunters and who had never before been photographed. Indeed, Cotlow's prophetic dream came true in glowing and successful reality!

Your dreams may be trying to point out future events, good or bad, in the symbology of your dreams. If you know how to interpret these dreams, you may avoid some tragedy in your own life or be able to help another person avoid misfortune.

A Dream of Fire Saved Her Husband's Life

The wife of a traveling salesman dreamed frequently of a fire in which people were trapped in the upper stories of a building and burned to death. She would awaken from this nightmare, fearful and apprehensive for her husband's safety. One night, after she had this dream, she called her husband, who was staying at the LaSalle Hotel in Chicago. She warned him that her dream had shown many people killed in a fire and cautioned him to be careful. A few days later, when her husband returned home, he told her that he had been awakened by the smell of smoke, and, forewarned by his wife's dreams, was able to rush out to safety. The LaSalle Hotel fire that night took more than 100 lives!

You can probe your dreams for warnings of danger that might threaten your or your family's future safety. Sometimes your dreams may be casting shadows of fear and anxiety that reveal themselves as nightmares from which you awaken in terror. Some common nightmares concern car accidents in which you may be trapped and unable to free yourself. A strange paralysis often accompanies these terror dreams, and you want to scream out but cannot. Or you may dream of being burned to death or being under water, unable to rise to the surface for breath. Sometimes these dreams are of shapeless monsters jumping out at you, ready to crush or devour you. Attempts at fleeing or screaming are usually blocked by a strange paralysis, which immobilizes you.

THE DR. JEKYLL AND MR. HYDE PERSONALITIES IN YOUR DREAMS

To understand this type of dream, it is necessary to know about the two distinct personalities that are in everyone's mind. This is a kind of Jekyll and Hyde thing in which one is trying to gain dominance over the other. The two forces are represented in all realms of nature as good opposed to evil; the devil opposed to God; sickness opposed to health; life opposed to death. When the dreams are of the type called "incubus attacks," they usually signify that the higher psychic nature is aware that we may be on a collision course in life that could produce sickness, accident, misery, and tragedy.

Marilyn Monroe's Dreams Drove Her to Suicide

The late Marilyn Monroe once told me in an interview that as a child she frequently had such dreams of terror in which monsters tried to devour her. In one such dream, she saw the devil, clothed in red, with real horns, carrying a pitchfork, as she had always pictured him, come toward her. She found herself terrified but could not scream out or run, as she seemed to be paralyzed. Then from a high mountain place, she said the devil offered her the world if she would worship him. She awakened before she found out what would have happened if she had fallen down to worship him. This dream, no doubt inspired by her childhood religious teaching about Jesus' being tempted by Satan in the wilderness, came to her frequently.

Marilyn Monroe then told me a startling story that her dreams seemed to have inspired. One night during a severe storm, with lightning flashing and thunder roaring, she went to the window of her room and thought: *If God is more powerful than the devil, then let Him strike me dead with the lightning!* When nothing happened to her, she said, "If the devil can give me beauty, fame, and fortune, I'll give him my soul when I die." Whether she told me this for shock effect or not, I don't know, but I never revealed this episode while she lived. When she committed suicide, I wondered if this strange bargain between her Jekyll and Hyde personalities, representing God and the devil, had finally triggered her subconscious to commit suicide. We'll never know, but in dreamology we do know that our dreams often influence our actions, shape our characters, and affect our destinies in strange ways.

In my dream analysis laboratory for several years, where our lecture members came to reveal their dreams and have them analyzed, I found several occurrences that seemed to point to our dreams being fantasy lives in which we act out our own suppressions, hostilities, desires, and aspirations. One side of the mind, let's call it the Hyde part, is out to destroy us and rob us of peace of mind and happiness. It wants us to fail, to become sick, to lose our money in stupid investments. The other side of the mind, the Jekyll part, paints a rosy picture of the future; it shows us living in a castle with our prince or princess; it reveals methods for finding a goldmine or oil deposits; it shows us riding in a Cadillac, gambling at Monte Carlo, relaxing on the Riviera, making love to beautiful women or men—in other words, it wants us to have a paradise on earth and seems to be trying to push us in the direction of fame, fortune, happiness, health, and riches.

Which side will win out in your dream dramas? The side that you consciously choose and the side you program into your own higher psychic mind centers.

REGIMEN TO PROGRAM YOUR HIGHER PSYCHIC MIND CENTERS

You can select the type of dreams you want to have and clothe them with characters, scenes, and even dialogue. You can demand that the evil Hyde evacuate your consciousness, leaving Dr. Jekyll to control the citadel of your dream consciousness. You can suggest that your "incubus attacks" of nightmares and terror leave your subconscious and be replaced by peaceful, relaxing, beautiful, and inspiring dreams.

Here is the method to use for creating your future with your dreams and letting your dreams "cast their shadows before."

1. When you have an especially disturbing nightmare, you will undoubtedly awake immediately and find yourself in a state of shock and outrage. Keep yourself from going back to sleep, turn on the lights, write down your nightmare in all its details, and then view it as a hidden attack of your Hyde personality. It may represent something you did, some moral infraction you committed, something you said to a friend or relative, some sexual act you performed that caused deep guilt. Whatever the cause, analyze it in this light; it is trying to punish you for your acts and make you feel guilty and inferior. You will then suggest to your subconscious, in simple words, something like this:

I know that my other half is trying to punish me for some moral infraction. I now disclaim this other half that represents the dark, morbid, and hateful side of my animal nature. I now imprint on my higher psychic mind thoughts of good, of health, of love, peace, beauty, and prosperity. I will incorporate all these elements into my dreams and they will accurately foreshadow my future life experiences.

2. After you have given yourself this type of suggestion, go back to sleep, and you will probably register in your dream world acts of courage, adventure, romance, and beauty. Your mental slate will be cleaned of the shadows that have plagued you in the past. You may then dream of making a fortune, of finding a goldmine, of doing some heroic act for which you are rewarded, showing that now you have firmly enthroned your Jekyll personality in the driver's seat and need no longer fear the Hyde part that is trying to destroy you.

3. Keep a "dream chart" on the nightstand by your bed to record your different dreams. Each night, when you go to bed, look at this dream chart and pick out the types of dreams that you have enjoyed and that gave you pleasure. Make up your mind that you are going to have similar dreams that night. Then look at the dreams that caused you concern and worry. Tell your subconscious, "I don't want any more of these bad dreams or nightmares." Then when you go to sleep, the last thing you think of will be, "My dreams tonight will be pleasant and beautiful, foreshadowing constructive and positive things to come."

A Girl's Dreams Told Her to Live Her Own Life

One woman in our dream laboratory told of how she kept a dream chart and what its results were in her life. She said, "I frequently had nightmares in which someone came to me with the news that my mother or father had died in a tragic accident. I would try to go to the place where they were, but something held me back, a kind of paralysis that made it impossible for me to move or scream out. The dream was so very real that I usually awakened in a state of shock. Sometimes I dreamed that I was buried alive, and I kept trying to cry out, 'Don't bury me, I'm alive, I'm alive!' I would try to move my hands or head but could not. I was completely unable to make a sound, and my body was paralyzed. I awakened from these dreams with a feeling of deep depression that carried all through the next day."

In the analysis section of our classes, we would attempt to find out the hidden causes of the frightening nightmares and explain them away, thus freeing the dreamer of future nightmares.

In this girl's case, we discovered that her mother and father had opposed her marriage to a Greek boy who worked in his father's restaurant. They lived in a little southern town where such "foreigners" were considered undesirable. She had run away with this boy and married him. When she returned to her town, her father and mother were so enraged that they forced the girl (who was still a minor) to annul her marriage. Now, at the age of twenty-five, she had never married or even fallen in love again.

I explained to this girl that her dreams of accidental deaths of her mother and father really represented a subconscious, buried desire to destroy them for having destroyed her marriage happiness. Being civilized, she could not face the thought of actually wanting to kill her parents, so she had her Hyde dream-self cause them to have an accident.

Being buried alive was another matter—her subconscious rage for having to live a life deprived of love and sex represented in her mind a state of being buried alive. Her dream-self was really trying to tell her, "You're burying your feelings and emotions; get out of your coffin and live again. Find someone you can love and marry, have a family of your own, and get out from under the domination of your parents."

The satisfying part of this dream analysis was that it worked. She did stop having her nightmares and met a young man in the dream analysis class who fell in love with her. They were married the following June.

4. Your conscious mind, the other half of the consciousness team that controls your life and dream world, has the ability to dictate to the other twin and even command it to obey its directions. This is why it is vitally important that you try to recall your dreams and write them down in a kind of Dream Diary. You may note that the dreams of tragedy, urgency, fear, and worry predominate in such a dream diary. These accurately parallel the periods of your life where there is stress and strain, where you are struggling with financial, romantic, or health problems. These dreams are trying to warn you to get out of the unfortunate circumstances that your psychic twin knows you are headed for.

The Hyde side of your consciousness is overjoyed when you

continue to have these recurring dreams of horror, for it feels it is the guardian of your morals and believes that you should be punished for your many infractions of the rules in the game of life.

This theme dominates our education, our religion, and our philosophy. The puritan idea that it is sinful to enjoy life is mirrored in the proverb "An idle mind is the devil's workshop." A few hundred years ago more than a million people were burned at the stake because they were believed to be witches. Our penal systems are based on the old Hebrew law "An eye for an eye." If we strive to become rich and successful we are told that "Love of money is the root of all evil" or "It is harder for a rich man to enter the kingdom of Heaven than for a camel to pass through the eye of a needle."

To avoid dreams of mental flagellation, you can program your psychic mind to the bright, joyous themes that you want to experience in your present and future life.

5. Instead of dwelling on your problems just before you drop off to sleep, pass through your memory all the happy experiences you have known, starting with your childhood. Mentally see your family gatherings at Thanksgiving and Christmas, where you felt emotionally secure and joyous. Think of your first circus, the first time you stood at the ocean's edge and watched a sunset; picture your first romance and the pleasure that it brought you. Think of the health and vitality you possess, and do not dwell on the times you had an operation or a broken bone.

Then as you stand at the threshold of that mysterious world between sleeping and waking, you will suddenly find yourself caught up in a roseate glow of the soul's joyous remembrances, which will be projected in the night's mosaic of dreams. Not only will you be programming your psychic mind with these pictures of happiness and beauty, but you will actually be conditioning your subconscious mind with the theme of health, happiness, and success, which will begin to manifest first in your dreams and then in the reality of your life experiences.

REVIEW OF POINTS IN CHAPTER FIVE

1. Our dreams accurately mirror our fears and anxieties, as well as our hopes and aspirations; these are couched in the universal symbols that dreams reflect in all their vividness.
2. You can train your psychic twin to bring you prophetic dreams that reveal the design of your future life.
3. A famous explorer was prodded into his new career by dreams that foretold it.
4. Your own dreams may be trying to protect you from some future danger or warn you of an impending tragedy.
5. The wife of a traveling salesman had a prophetic dream of fire. He was in the ill-fated LaSalle Hotel in Chicago the night of the tragic fire that took many lives, but because of his wife's warnings he escaped unharmed.
6. By knowing the Jekyll and Hyde sides of your psychic twins, you can program the forces that represent good, health, life, and prosperity and avoid the evils of sickness, death, accident, and misfortune.
7. Marilyn Monroe had terrifying dreams of the devil offering her the world if she would worship him. She succumbed to this temptation in a weird pact with the "devil" force of her evil psychic twin and was destroyed through suicide.
8. You can program the Jekyll character in your dream world and cause it to reveal methods for finding riches, making a business successful, being happy in love with your true soul mate, and bringing many other pleasures and rewards.
9. You can program your higher psychic mind centers with the dreams that provide you the setting for achieving your high goals and aspirations.
10. Nightmares are usually attempts by the Hyde power to punish you for moral infractions.
11. By making a dream chart you can program your higher mind with dreams that give you pleasure and that you wish repeated.
12. Dreams of suffocation, drowning, being buried alive, and other paralyzing dreams are trying to reveal some deep, hidden subconscious fact that causes one pain and misery.

13. A woman in our dream analysis laboratory had such dreams that revealed her hatred of her mother and father for breaking up her marriage with a man she truly loved.

14. You can learn how to avoid dreams of mental flagellation that have been implanted by wrong education or religious training.

6

CREATE A NEW SELF-IMAGE, FREE OF GUILT, INFERIORITY, AND FAILURE COMPLEXES

Most people suffer from an inferiority complex in one way or another. Many of us experience emotional insecurity because we had childhoods where we were made to feel our inferiority and dependence on our parents or other family members.

We find ourselves going through life whistling in the dark to give ourselves confidence and a feeling of safety. However, lurking in the shadows of our subconscious there are frightening creatures—sickness, accident, premature death, and eternal oblivion—that threaten to destroy us.

CHILDHOOD TRAINING HANG-UPS

These shadows that darken our dream world with fearsome specters are often due to the wrong childhood training that suppressed our personalities. We are told, "Young people should be seen and not heard." We are commanded to obey no matter how we may feel that to do so is not compatible with our own innate desires. Every move we make in the first years of life seems to bring a reprimand or a warning. Our subconscious minds are programmed with injunctions: "Don't touch that. Be careful! You'll be hurt. Don't break the lamp. Watch out you don't fall. Be careful not to eat things that hurt you. Don't go near the fire.

Don't touch chemicals in bottles or open medicine chests. Stay away from the water; you'll drown. Don't trust people; they'll kidnap you or harm you. Don't get your feet wet or you'll catch your death of cold. Don't eat so fast; you'll choke to death. Go to sleep or the bogey man will get you. Watch out—if you're not good the policeman will come and take you away in a big black bag."

Even our fairytales are filled with giants, witches, and other evil beings. Jack and Jill came to disaster when they merely climbed the hill "to get a pail of water." Hansel and Gretel were fattened by the witch so that she could feast on them. Rumpelstiltskin split in half in an alarming manner, and Humpty Dumpty could not be put back together by "all the king's horses and all the king's men."

Is it any wonder that many children wake up screaming in nightmares brought on by these violent childhood warnings and fantasies?

THE FOUR VITAL URGES TO PROGRAM INTO YOUR SUBCONSCIOUS

There are four urges that mold our mental and physical lives. These urges, when correctly used, can shape our consciousness in such a way that we become self-reliant, confident, poised, and success-oriented. When any of them is lacking or improperly used, we are subject to mental and emotional conflicts, sickness, poverty, and general misfortune. Our dreams are then filled with the shadow-forms that predict our nervous breakdowns, accidents, and disasters in future life. Incorporate these four urges in your dream consciousness.

1. The Life Urge
2. The Power Urge
3. The Success Urge
4. The Love Urge

THE LIFE URGE

If you wish to have good health throughout your life, to remain youthful and live to be 100 years or more, you must use the life urge and imprint it on your psychic mind centers. It will then transmit its impulses to your sympathetic nervous system, giving your brain and body vitality and increasing your chances of being healthy and remaining young.

When your psychic centers are programmed with this life urge your dreams will generally reflect cheerful, optimistic, and even joyous subject matter. You will have no nightmares that involve you in scenes of horror and death. If you persistently dream of serious diseases, operations, hospitals, and things related to death such as funerals, coffins, or other death symbols, the psychic mind might be trying to warn you that something is drastically wrong with some organ of your body.

Onassis Lost the Will to Live after His Son's Tragic Death

A close friend of the Greek shipping magnate Aristotle Onassis told me that a year before his son's death Onassis had frightening nightmares in which some dreadful thing was happening that he could not control. One such dream was that one of his ships was afire and he was a young seaman on the ship, locked in a compartment below decks from which he could not escape. His screams for help brought no response, and when he awoke he felt that something frightening was going to happen to him. Soon after that time, he suffered an affliction of his eyes that threatened him with blindness; then there was a fire on one of his ships in which several crewmen were injured; and finally, the loss of his only son in an airplane crash! He confided to his friend after this tragedy that he no longer had a desire to live and that he would give all of his vast fortune for the life of his son. A year later Onassis was dead. When the urge to live fails us, we are given premonitions of coming shadows of disaster, and finally the cells of the brain and body begin to deteriorate and disintegrate.

How to Know If You Are Courting Disaster through Your Dreams

If you persistently dream of certain forms of disaster, or have recurring dream symbols relating to age, sickness, and death, you will realize that your higher psychic mind is trying to warn you of future disasters.

One woman in our dream analysis laboratory told of having a persistent dream of a snake coiled around her body, crushing her, and when she was paralyzed with fear and unable to call out for help, the snake attempted to crawl into her vagina. She experienced such terror from this dream that after awaking she would remain awake until dawn, fearful that the dream might repeat itself.

It was soon after this terrifying dream that she began to have regular periods of bleeding from the uterus, and upon examination by a specialist, it was found that she had cancer of the uterus. Her psychic twin was trying to give her a warning of something wrong with her in that area of her body and had she early enough taken these dream symbols seriously, she might have avoided tragedy.

If you often dream that your teeth are all falling out, this could be a warning that you face some physical disfigurement that you fear, or that you are worried about growing old, or losing your sex appeal, or attractiveness. In men this type of dream is often symbolically expressing the fear that they are losing their potency or masculinity.

If you have frequent dreams of fire, they could be warnings of actual danger through future fires, or they may be symbolical dreams showing the need for purification or cleansing of the body's internal organs. You may be eating the wrong things and your psychic twin is trying to warn you that you should go on a diet, to save yourself from obesity and the accompanying symptoms of high blood pressure, strokes, and heart attacks.

A Dream Warned a Man of an Impending Stroke

A man I once counseled told me that he had a dream of being at a Fourth of July celebration. He was enjoying the fireworks display, with shooting rockets and showers of starlike firebursts against the night sky. But suddenly fear overcame him as an unusually large rocket exploded, showering him with flames that seemed to engulf the upper part of his shoulders and head. He awoke screaming with fear.

A few weeks later this man experienced a sudden bursting of a blood vessel in his brain that left him paralyzed and unable to speak or walk. His overburdened psyche, sensing that it was time for a mental and physical explosion, had been trying to warn this man of an impending stroke.

Do not wait for some misfortune to occur before taking action. Search the symbolical meanings of your dreams carefully and find clues that will give you warnings in plenty of time to take steps to protect your health and your life.

Each night when you go to bed, program your psychic centers with the following life urge suggestions.

I wish to implement the life urge within my mind and body. I shall live a balanced life, avoiding stresses and strains that might make me ill. I imprint my subconscious with the urge to be healthy, to be young, and to live 100 years or more.

How Life Can Be Prolonged through Dream Programming

A woman who was building a home with her husband of many years suddenly experienced a tragedy. Her husband died suddenly and she was left alone. She had no desire now to finish the magnificent home that they had planned together. She had been left a large amount of money, for her husband was the founder of the Winchester firearms fortune. But now she was sad and lonely, with little urge to live.

One night Mrs. Winchester had a vivid dream in which she and her husband were strolling through a newly built home like young honeymooners. There were many rooms, winding staircases, porches, and courtyards. As they stopped to admire the house her husband began to fade away like a ghost image and she heard his voice say, "When the house is finished you will join me, my darling." She awakened with a start, and while the dream was still vivid in her mind, she made up her mind that, in some mysterious way, her husband was trying to warn her that she would die when the home was finished. She then made up her mind that she would continue building the house as long as possible, believing that thus her own life would be somehow prolonged.

That dream turned out to be prophetic; the house kept growing bigger and bigger; hundreds of rooms spread out over acres of land. Stairways led to nowhere; doors and windows opened up on vacant space; chimneys and fireplaces sprouted all over the place. As the years passed, the building kept getting bigger and bigger, and Mrs. Winchester remained healthy and strong, even though she reached an advanced age. Finally, after many years, and after spending millions of dollars on a home she would never live in, Mrs. Winchester lost the will to live. She finished the house and quietly lay down and died.

THE POWER URGE

There are various forms of power that we are all trying to express. Some men, like former President Nixon, are never satisfied until they have reached the highest office in the land. Others want to express power through money, and we find people like Howard Hughes, Aristotle Onassis, W. Clement Stone, J. Paul Getty, and the Rockefellers, spending their lifetime energies to build vast financial empires that will survive them.

Ego recognition is one form of this power urge that is in all of us to some degree. We wish to win recognition for our work, to be adequately rewarded with money or other equivalents, to be loved and to love, to have social recognition, and to win the plaudits of the world for the great things we achieve.

How to Build a Strong Ego Urge for Greater Power

You can discover if your power or ego urge is strong enough or too weak by the symbols of your dreams. Those who have strong, well-defined egos, with plenty of success drive, are usually people who have been trained by their parents to believe they are superior beings. They are the college graduates who think that by virtue of a diploma they are going to conquer the world and somehow possess extraordinary and superior powers of the mind. In fact, psychological records show that 65 percent of all college graduates do usually succeed in achieving their goals in life, whereas the percentage is much lower in cases of those who have had only a high school or grammar school education.

Ego power urges are easy to spot in your dreams. If you dream frequently of certain events or symbols, then your ego urge is strong and needs no further suggestions. These events or symbols can be of the following nature:

Dreams in which the dreamer is a member of royalty, or where the symbol of the crown predominates, could signify that the person's ego is very strong and that he longs for recognition, fame, success, and fortune. It is said of Napoleon that he was a great believer in dreams and that his recurring dream was that he would be crowned emperor of France, and this finally led to the fulfillment of what could have been a delusional ego trip for another.

THE SUCCESS URGE

The success urge goes together with the power or ego urge. When the ego drive is well defined and strong, the individual's dreams are rosy, optimistic, and joyous, and he has few dreams of anxiety or "incubus attacks."

If a person has frequent dreams of being a hero who is being acclaimed or being given a ticker-tape parade, it is more than likely that his ego is trying to push him in the direction of fame and worldly acclaim. This does not necessarily mean that he will achieve them; he could make the effort to succeed and still fail.

Maria Callas's Secret Dream

I recall one summer when I was visiting on the Greek Riviera, and a friend at the American Embassy invited me to a party aboard Onassis's yacht. At that party there were three world-famous personalities who had already achieved acclaim in their individual fields. Two of them—Elizabeth Taylor and Greta Garbo—I had met before when I was known as the adviser to the Hollywood stars. The other celebrity was Maria Callas, the great opera star who is thought by many to have one of the greatest voices in the world. These three women had what I call the "magic circle" of success, a magnetic aura that radiated about them, like golden light, giving them the power to attract and hold people. The conversation came around to mystic things and astral projection. Maria Callas told the gathering that when she was a youngster in Athens, she and her mother were very poor, often not having enough to eat. She had frequent dreams that she was standing on the stage of a huge amphitheater, singing to thousands of people. Up above she could see a full, silvery moon, and the end of her song was greeted by a standing ovation.

Then she continued, "I often used to sit on the Hill of the Muses directly opposite the glistening white marble Parthenon. I would watch the tourists struggling up the Acropolis, to stand in awe before one of the most perfect buildings in the world. I would recall my dreams of singing and winning worldwide acclaim, and I told myself that some day the world would come to hear me sing. I vowed to train my voice so that in my way I would be as perfect as the Parthenon was. That dream and that resolve never left me in all the years that I struggled to achieve success as a singer."

Only a few years before I met Maria Callas I had been present in the magnificent theater below the Parthenon, on a night when there was a full moon, and I heard the great singer in a concert program that brought the audience to its feet for a thunderous ovation. It was truly a dream come true, and I felt privileged to witness this triumph.

Strong Ego Dreams

If your dreams reflect ego power, it is likely that you find yourself being acclaimed for something great you have achieved. Or you may find yourself flying when everyone else is earthbound, and the mortals below look up at you in stunned amazement.

Perhaps your dreams show you being a conquering general in some ancient period. Or if you are a woman, you may be on a throne like Marie Antoinette. Sometimes this well-developed ego will masquerade as a famous modern personality like Elizabeth Taylor and show her living in a beautiful mansion with dozens of servants waiting on her. If it is a man, he may become Robert Redford in his dreams, making love to beautiful women and seeing himself mobbed by hordes of autograph seekers.

Ego-recognition dreams are frequent in those who are well integrated and suffer no qualms from inferiority feelings, self-consciousness, and inadequacy. In such dreams your psychic twin may be trying to say to you, "You're great, you know. Keep on trying, for the world will finally recognize the great genius you are and reward you with fame and riches."

Weak Ego Dreams

Those who are not so fortunate as to have this ego urge highly developed, and who consequently suffer from pangs of inferiority and inadequacy, often have dreams that show them as an underdog in life, taking orders, being in servile positions, and suffering humiliation, poverty, and degradation.

One boy of thirteen had frequent dreams in which he wore a dunce cap in school and sat in a corner, while other children taunted and jeered at him. An examination showed that he had deep-seated feelings of inferiority brought about by a drunken father who frequently beat him and told him that he would never amount to anything. This boy required months of psychotherapy to rid him of his nightmares and to help him overcome his tendencies to feelings of inferiority and self-consciousness.

A man had dreams that he was climbing to reach some unknown height when he slipped, stumbled, and fell down again. No matter how hard he tried, he could never scale the heights and achieve his objective. This was clearly an ego-frustrating type of dream that showed his feelings of inadequacy and fears of failure. He had to be reprogrammed with the winning qualities of self-reliance and self-confidence before he could go out and succeed in his chosen profession.

Sometimes these dreams of weak egos will show the person falling into quicksand and being sucked under. Or he will be swimming against the tide, and no matter how hard he tries, he will still be carried downstream. One man who was an admitted failure in his personal, as well as his business, life had a disquieting dream in which he was a helpless bird and an eagle swooped down and carried him off. When the symbology of this dream was pointed out to him, he changed his self-image from a cringing, inferior type of person to one who believed in himself. Soon he was working in a new company that gave him a responsible position at very good pay.

THE LOVE URGE

Despite Freud's early assumptions that everything in dreams related in some way to this strong emotion and the sex nature, modern studies in dreamology indicate that this is not true. Everything in connection with dreams is not related to sex or love, but this emotion does play a vitally important part in every person's life, and sex-oriented dreams and fantasies are often clearly marked off from all other types of dreams.

When the love urge is strong, normal, and well balanced, the dreams are usually of happy events in connection with members of the opposite sex. One may dream of marriage, of having a family of three or four children, of the wedding night with its anxieties, but also its joys. Or the symbols may be churches, wedding cakes, bridal gowns, the ringing of bells, the crossing of a bridge, or two roads that lead in different directions (signifying that marriage will lead one in a different direction).

Frustration in Love Can Lead to Mental and Physical Breakdowns

When the love urge is suppressed and there is frustration and unhappiness, the dreams suddenly take on bizzare and often unintelligible patterns. The person who expresses his love nature freely, without guilt or shame, is generally free of these strange dreams. Some symbols that masquerade in these frustration dreams are well known to dreamologists as phallic symbols, such as a candle, banana, arrow, sword, or gun.

Phallic symbols are usually represented in strange ways. A woman who was analyzed in our dream laboratory was a spinster at forty, with little prospect of ever finding a husband, although she confessed she had tried. Her dreams were mixed and usually filled with these strange symbols. As she was highly moral and puritanical, her psychic twin avoided such obvious language as guns, bananas, or swords. She often dreamed that she was a child, holding a candle in her hand, searching for something in a big house. She never found the object of her search though she looked in all the likely places, and always felt a keen sense of disappointment when it eluded her again and again. She also dreamed of a church in which candles burned brightly at the altar. She was standing there, dressed in a bridal gown of pure white, waiting for the bridegroom, whose face was always concealed, and just as he approached to take the marriage vows, the wedding turned into a funeral and she saw herself lying in the casket, still dressed in her bridal gown. Of course, this dream represented her psychic twin's desire to have her marry, and yet her frustrations showed themselves in the fact that she "buried" her hopes and dreams in a graveyard of oblivion.

Dreams in which a person is shooting arrows into the air at some unknown object always represent the symbol of Cupid shooting his arrows into a lover's heart. Guns and swords and knives that play an important part in dreams usually relate to a person's suppressed desires and aspirations relating to love and marriage.

Dream fantasies in which a person is carrying out the act of love with a phantom lover usually represent the normal desires that are in every person. If the dreams are weird or ususual in any respect, they could be indications that something is wrong in one's sex life and one's psychic twin is trying to bring about changes for the better.

A Woman Dreamed of Having an Affair with the Devil

One woman had frequent dreams that she was having sex with a handsome, young lover, only to suddenly find that he was covered with hair all over his body. When she looked up at his face, she saw a diabolical expression on it and two horns sprouting on his forehead. She revealed in our dream analysis that as a young woman she had been forcibly raped and had feared relations with men from that time on. She never told her husband this but kept the secret suppressed within herself. To her psychic twin all men were "devils" and she confessed that she had never had an orgasm and found the sex act "beastly and unpleasant."

Although she had two children, she was not a wife to her husband in the true sense. When this dream was analyzed and openly discussed, the woman lost some of her dread of sex, and later admitted to me in private consultation that she was beginning to enjoy her love relationship for the first time in her life and several times had been aroused to orgasm.

REVIEW OF POINTS IN CHAPTER SIX

1. You can handle emotional insecurity, inferiority, and feelings of guilt and self-consciousness by subconscious reprogramming.
2. Many children receive negative training, forbidding them to express their own natures and find their own paths to emotional security.
3. The four urges that shape our dream consciousness are the life urge, the power urge, the success urge, and the love urge.
4. Aristotle Onassis had frightening dreams that occured before the loss of his only son. His dreams also accurately foreshadowed his own decline and death.
5. You can learn the dream symbols that may foretell tragedy.
6. One woman in dream analysis reported that she frequently dreamed of a snake trying to crush her, and this terrifying dream led to the discovery that she had cancer.
7. To dream of teeth falling out signifies that one fears sexual impotency, losing one's sex appeal, or aging.
8. A man dreamed of fireworks that exploded on his head and shoulders, burning him; later he had a paralyzing stroke.
9. You can program your psychic centers with life urge suggestions to make you stay healthy and live a long life.
10. A woman dreamed that she would die when she finished her home; for years she kept building a huge, rambling structure. She did die upon completion of her home, which was never occupied.
11. You can learn how to use the ego-recognition power urge to win recognition in your work, build a fortune, and achieve fulfillment in a career.

12. Greek opera star Maria Callas used her childhood dreams of fame and fortune to become a great singer.

13. You can learn how to interpret your ego-recognition dreams and overcome self-consciousness, inferiority, and inadequacy in your personal and business life.

14. You can use the love urge to bring you new joys and satisfaction in your love relationships without fear, guilt, or worry.

7
HOW DAYDREAMS AND PSYCHIC SOMNAMBULISM CAN SHAPE DESTINY

You need not always be asleep when you dream. You can dream with your eyes wide open and use a process known in mysticism as Psychic Somnambulism to work out your dream fantasies, project them into your future, and make them living realities.

Many great men and women used this dream technique to create their destinies and discover secrets in nature that helped change the course of history.

Napoleon Changed the Course of History through His Dreams

Napoleon lived in a state of psychic somnambulism a great deal of the time. After he had led his armies to victory and had dreamed prophetically of being emperor of France, he began to prepare for that historic day by a typical act of psychic somnambulism. He called in the great tragedian Talma and told him that he wished to be shown how to look and act the part of an emperor. As the Corsican was only about five feet tall, he realized that he must adopt a commanding posture that would inspire respect and admiration in his subjects. Talma put a book on Napoleon's head and told him to imagine it was a crown of pure gold studded with precious jewels. Then he told Napoleon to walk back and forth in his tent on the edge of the battlefield, saying aloud, "I am Emperor Napoleon the First." He repeated this over and over. Talma also told him to imagine that he was dressed in a royal purple cloak, trimmed with ermine. He showed him how to stand erect with his head held high, a position that added inches to his stature. As Napoleon fantasized that he was an emperor, he was automatically programming his higher psychic centers with the power of command and control over the destinies of millions of people.

You can use psychic somnambulism in your own life to program your psychic centers with dreams of success, money, fame, love-happiness, health, joy, friendship, and fulfillment of your every dream. Your daydreams can be harnessed to create a great destiny, to release creative gifts and talents. In other words, you can become anything you want and do anything you really believe you can do if you use this self-hypnotic power of psychic somnambulism to program your higher mind.

REGIMEN TO TURN YOUR DAYDREAMS INTO REALITY

1. Make it a point each day to sit in reverie and meditate on the dream world you wish to create. When you close your eyes and go into meditation, there is a state of awareness that gives you superior psychic powers and sharpens your senses. You will then project onto the psychic screen of your mind, in vivid picture form, the work you wish to do, the type of business you want to own, the soul mate you wish to attract, the house you want to live in, the social life you desire, the countries you would like to visit. In fact, you can project each day several daydreams onto this psychic screen, with an emotion of intensity, and the feeling that you are acting out the dream and making it a living reality.

Charles Lindbergh's Early Dreams of Flying Brought Success

I once met Charles Lindbergh after he became world famous with his flight to Paris. It was at the home of George Palmer Putnam, who had published my first book. I saw the copy of the check for $175,000 that Putnam had given to Lindbergh in royalties. After dinner the talk turned to the motivation behind Lindbergh's perilous voyage on that memorable day. He said, "When I was a young child, I used to often sit alone and daydream. I would look up at the blue skies and see birds floating gracefully in the summer sunshine, and I found myself thinking, *How wonderful it would be if I could fly like a bird.* Then later, when aviation had advanced and I was still in my teens, I had vivid dreams in which I saw myself flying in an airplane, to strange, unknown lands and returning safely. I always had an exhilarated feeling when I was in these dream states, and I believe that these daydreams furnished the motivation for my interest in aviation."

2. After you have sat for a while in these states of reverie, projecting your future actions onto the psychic screen of your higher mind, begin to act and feel as if you are already fulfilling your dreams. If you project riches and success, feel successful, go to expensive hotels and sit in the lobby and absorb the atmosphere of luxury and wealth. Visit art galleries and steep yourself in the beauty of paintings and statues; try to imagine how the artists created these masterpieces through their daydreams of beauty and perfection. Study biographies of people who achieved great things in art, music, literature, invention, science, and industry; try to take on their thoughts, their dreams of future greatness, until your mind is so saturated with inspiration that you will dare to dream big and achieve for yourself a great destiny.

Conrad Hilton Built a Hotel Empire through His Dreams

I have a photograph, which I prize very highly, that shows me talking with the great hotel magnate Conrad Hilton at my Bel-Air home. He told me of his early struggles when he was a young man in a small Texas city. He often sat in periods of reverie and projected the dream that he would one day become a hotel man and own the Waldorf Astoria, one of the luxury hotels in New York City. This dream led Hilton to study everything he could learn about hotel management, and even his night dreams were filled with visions of luxury hotels that would bear his name in all corners of the globe.

A few years later, Conrad Hilton bought the Waldorf Astoria

and that set the stage for building his vast hotel empire that has spread around the world.

3. You can shape your daydreams and fantasies into any channel you choose, and soon you will be acting like a sleepwalker, carrying out your dreams in living reality. That is what the term *psychic somnambulism* means in mysticism; you begin to be guided by your higher psychic mind, your higher twin that knows all, sees all, and is all, to fulfilling the destiny you are projecting. Somnambulism refers to the act of sleepwalking. A person walking in his sleep can be on a fifteenth story ledge and never fall off. But if he is awakened suddenly, he may fall to his death. In fact, a true story exemplifies how a person can do amazing things when in this state of psychic somnambulism, which is literally a kind of hypnotic trance.

Psychic Somanambulism Caused a Girl to Swim while Asleep

A young woman disappeared each night around midnight and returned later with her clothes all wet. One night her parents followed her to see where she went. The girl walked to a nearby lake where she plunged in and swam towards the other shore. The parents became alarmed, as they knew that their daughter could not swim in her waking state, and the mother called out a warning. The girl awakened from her somnambulistic state and drowned!

Use positive statements each night just before you drift off into your dream world to program your higher psychic centers with affirmative actions. Say each of these statements several times, or make up your own positive suggestions.

I can achieve anything I wish to achieve.

I am successful. I am going to become famous and rich.

I am perfect. I am valuable and will win recognition.

I am a loving person and I attract love-happiness.

I will myself to overcome any negative habits I may have.

I dare to dream big and achieve greatness.

I desire the unfolding of creative gifts so that I may paint great pictures (here mention any creative talent you desire, such as writing, composing, inventing, or having a business of your own).

4. After programming yourself in this way for a short time, start to act out the part you have cast yourself in; be sure it is a hero, not a villain. In your dreams try to be a romantic lover, not a frustrated, miserable failure. Act with a commanding presence, not a cringing, apologetic attitude that proclaims your feelings of inferiority and inadequacy. Assume the posture of a successful person; act as though you have a million dollars in the bank. In fact, to make this dream fantasy more realistic, actually carry a check made out to yourself for one million dollars. Sign the check God the Universal Banker. Each time you feel that you are poor and money does not seem to flow readily, look at that check and remind your dream-self that you have a million dollars worth of health; you possess the beauty of nature; you can enjoy free public parks, libraries, and museums; the public transportation systems are yours for a few cents a day; you can press a button on your TV or radio set and command a million-dollar performance from Elizabeth Taylor as Cleopatra, or have great comedians like Bob Hope, Milton Berle, and Johnny Carson perform for you. When you get tired of them, like a potentate you can cause them to vanish into thin air and tune in other great personalities.

5. Each night, just before you go to sleep, tell your psychic twin that rules your dream world that you want information for carrying out your waking dream fantasies and making them a living reality. Soon your dreams will become peopled with important, famous, and rich people. You will find yourself living in mansions and walking with kings; you will spend money as lavishly as a billionaire, and your life will reflect the ultimate joy of happiness in romance, fulfillment in your career, and a vital, happy body that will live for 100 years or more.

A Great Juliet Dreamed Herself to Fame

I once met a young actress backstage in a Broadway production of *Romeo and Juliet*. Her name was Claire Bloom. She told me that as a child of seven her mother took her to see *Romeo and Juliet* in London. The great drama made such an impression on her sensitive young mind that she decided she would one day be one of the greatest Juliets ever to appear on the stage. This dream fantasy stayed with Claire Bloom for years; she memorized the entire play of *Romeo and Juliet,* learning all the parts. Shakespeare became her idol, and she sat in reverie each day visualizing herself being Juliet. This dream came true for the beautiful young actress who has been acclaimed by critics as one of the greatest Juliets of our day!

REVIEW OF POINTS IN CHAPTER SEVEN

1. The mystical power of psychic somnambulism can help you dream with your eyes wide open and project those dreams into living reality, shaping your future destiny.
2. Napoleon used this secret technique to shape his future when he asked the tragedian Talma to show him how to look, talk, and act like an emperor.
3. You can learn how to use psychic somnambulism to program your own psychic centers with dreams of success, money, love-happiness, fame, friendship, and fulfillment of your every dream.
4. Psychic meditation can imprint your daydreams onto your psychic screen and project them to the outer world.
5. Charles Lindbergh once told me that as a child he had daydreams of flying like a bird, which motivated him to take up aviation in later years.
6. Carry out your dreams and fantasies in real life; feel successful; act like a rich person; become as brilliant, witty, and beautiful as you have programmed your psychic dream state to be.
7. Conrad Hilton used psychic somnambulism to build his vast hotel empire around the world.
8. The positive programming statements *I am, I can, I will, I dare,* and *I do* will imprint your psychic mind with desires that shape your future destiny.
9. Act the role of a romantic hero, not the part of a villain, in your life. Carry a check for one million dollars in your pocket and feel as rich as Midas. Take over public parks as your estates, museums and art galleries for your drawing rooms—be a billionaire in your dreams!
10. The great actress Claire Bloom acted out the dream of the perfect Juliet in her early years, and she was later acclaimed as one of the greatest Juliets of all time.

8
HOW MILLIONAIRES DREAMED THEMSELVES INTO THEIR FORTUNES

In writing my book *The Million Dollar Secret Hidden in Your Mind,* I once interviewed several millionaires to discover their secrets for building their fortunes. I found out that most of them had projected in their dream fantasies the desire that they would one day become successful and rich. Each one told me the secret dreams he had as a youngster, and it seemed always to be that they wanted to do something for the world, for their families, for humanity in general, rather than just to make money for its own sake.

SUCCESSFUL PEOPLE WHO DAYDREAMED OF GREATNESS

Most successful people spent a great deal of time daydreaming. They admit that even their nightly dreams were filled with visions of success in which they saw themselves achieving great things, money pouring in, and the world acclaiming them and their creative ideas.

Aristotle Onassis

When Aristotle Onassis was a young man, he once told me he worked as a deckhand on merchant ships. He helped pack goods in the huge cargo ships that went to America, South America, and ports in all parts of the world. After his work was finished, he would often sit on deck, relaxing and daydreaming. He always projected the dream that one day he would have ships voyaging to all parts of the world.

His dreams were filled with visions of himself on luxury yachts, entertaining rich and important people. In these dreams he saw himself conversing intelligently with those who had college educations, and even though he was not an intellectual, he dreamed himself as cultured, suave, and polished. His psychic twin was trying to steer him to the great destiny that was to be his.

Andrew Carnegie

As a poor boy in Scotland, Andrew Carnegie had frequent dreams that he would one day go to America and become rich and successful. He did not know how or when, but deep within his heart he knew that his dreams of wealth would one day be realized.

Charles Revson

Early in his career, Charles Revson had the dream of creating beauty aids for women. He had just begun his Revlon beauty company when I met him, and he told me, "Even as a young man I admired beauty in women. I wanted in some way to bring to women all over the world higher standards of beauty culture that would enhance their natural appearance." His dreams came true when he founded the Revlon beauty products company, which made him enormously rich and more importantly, fulfilled his dream of making women even more attractive and desirable.

Daydreams often shape our nightly world and cause us to act out the parts we have chosen to play on the stage of life. In dreams we frequently receive the psychic stimulation to invent some useful object, to compose beautiful music, to write great stories, to paint magnificent canvasses, to discover a scientific formula that will benefit the world.

Eli Whitney

A strange series of events brought Eli Whitney to the invention of his cotton gin, which changed the industry of the South. Whitney had a pet canary and also a pet cat. One evening as he dozed before his fireplace, he heard the frantic squeaking of his canary, and when he rushed to the cage, he saw his cat reaching in through the bars of the cage to catch the canary. As the bars were too closely spaced to permit the bird's body to go through, the cat only got a pawful of feathers. As Whitney sat before his fireplace again, in reverie, the idea suddenly came to him for the invention of the cotton gin. He saw iron bars, with narrow spaces between them, and an iron claw going in between the bars, catching the cotton, and pulling it out, while the cotton seeds remained behind the iron bars. This idea for the cotton gin was destined to change the course of history.

Robert Fulton

The American inventor Robert Fulton had a dream in which he saw water heated to a high degree, furnishing steam to move engines. He even dreamed up the idea of a steam torpedo, which would sail under water and sink enemy ships. He went to Napoleon with this idea, but the conqueror of all of Europe except England could not see its value. With that steam torpedo, Napoleon could have sunk all the British frigates that were in the harbor across the English Channel, and Napoleon might have been the ruler of the world!

Business Dreamers

The vision of a world on wheels put B. F. Goodrich's dream into action when he perfected tires for America's new cars.

William Wrigley had dreamed of riches and fame, and it spurred him into the discovery and manufacture of gum, which made him a fortune.

Louis Liggett had dreams of healing a sick world, and his psychic twin gave him ideas for establishing drug chains that made him rich.

The two partners who got the idea of mail-order merchandising for those who lived in rural areas and could not get to big department stores formed the Sears Roebuck Company from a dream that they both had in their early years.

The dream, which became his magnificent obsession, that he would one day create the most perfect car in the world, drove a man on to invent the Rolls Royce. He found a partner with plenty of money, and together they formed a company to produce cars that have become the symbol of elegance, riches, and perfection.

Throughout history, a dream has preceded the creation of something that benefited humanity or led to great discoveries in science, medicine, art, music, literature, or industry.

Behind every big company that provides services to the world there was someone's dream that came into glorious reality. IBM was founded by Tom Watson, who dreamed of bringing electronics into industry to improve efficiency and increase production. His motto, which was written on a card over every desk in the IBM building was the single word THINK. Your dreams project thought into its creative manifestations, and your psychic twin will dream up the methods by which you can achieve the fulfillment of your dreams of riches, fame, and success.

Such companies as Ford, General Motors, American Telephone and Telegraph, Bethlehem Steel, United States Steel, Chrysler, and Exxon—all of these great organizations came from the crystallized dreams of men and women who had big dreams and who achieved big success.

REGIMEN FOR TURNING YOUR DREAMS OF SUCCESS INTO REALITY

1. There is a formula that I have given to thousands of lecture members throughout the country, it is: *Dream, Dare, and Do.* Dream the big dream. Have the big, bold idea that you can achieve the great success you desire. Program this vivid dream

into your psychic mind centers by constant repetition of the thought that you will become rich, famous, and world renowned if that is your desire.

Your higher psychic mind centers will then become so programmed with these creative and inspiring ideas of success that they will magnetize your brain and literally make it a money magnet.

His Dreams of Empire Brought Him Health and Fortune

Cecil Rhodes was a very sick youngster, given up by doctors to die. He had tuberculosis, and in those days of the nineteenth century there was no known cure for the disease. He kept repeating his desire over and over, "I will live. I will become famous and rich. I will found an empire that will bear my name."

He daydreamed himself into health and riches. In those hours of lying in bed, waiting to die, he found the strength and courage to dream of future greatness.

Under the impetus of this magnificent obsession, his psychic twin gave him the idea of going to Africa to regain his health and to make his fortune. While in Africa he became healed, and founded his empire of 15,000 acres of beautiful land. He cultivated the land, and in so doing, discovered a diamond field that made him a multimillionaire. When he died, he left a bequest to establish the Rhodes scholarship at Oxford University.

2. If you dream continually about defeats, disappointments, poverty, and sickness, then you have been negatively programmed. You can change the content of your consciousness and soon your dreams will reflect your optimism, the expectation of good things, and will furnish you with the psychic drive to achieve your life goals.

A Producer's Dream Made Great Movies

I once met the famous producer Gabriel Pascal at a party in Hollywood. He had brought the then new star Greer Garson with him, and Pascal, Greer, her mother, and I remained long after the other guests had gone, talking about psychic phenomena, dreams, and other fascinating subjects dealing with mystical experiences.

Pascal believed in astral projection, reincarnation, and the soul's ability to project itself during one's sleeping state to discover secrets of the universe, to communicate with those on other planes of consciousness, and to reach into the minds of others to influence and control them.

He told of how he had frequent dreams over the years that he would become famous and rich, but the method of doing so was always concealed from him. He saw himself being entertained by kings and presidents; he visualized the life he would have as a worldwide traveler; and he knew, in his dreams, that this would all come about in some way through the medium of motion pictures.

One day, as he sat in meditation, his psychic twin gave him a sudden jolt. "I want you to get the motion picture rights to all of George Bernard Shaw's stage plays," it told him. Pascal said he argued back, "But I haven't any way of reaching Shaw. I have no money, no background, and even if I got to him he would probably throw me out of the house. I know how bad-tempered he is and how he has turned down millions of dollars from motion picture producers for his plays."

But his psychic twin would not give up; it kept prodding Pascal with this idea until he finally gave in and decided he would try to reach Shaw.

Not having the bus fare to go into the country where Shaw lived, Pascal hitchhiked all the way to Shaw's sumptuous estate many miles from London. When he arrived he was tongue-tied, certain he could not say a single word. But when the butler opened the door, he suddenly found something taking over his mind and speaking through him. He listened in amazement as the butler admitted him and told him to follow him into Mr. Shaw's study.

When Pascal found himself before the great playwright, he was cringing in fear, but his psychic twin took over once more and he heard himself saying, "Mr. Shaw, I have long admired your great plays and I think it's time for the entire world to be able to see your genius through the medium of motion pictures."

Shaw started to speak, but Pascal silenced him with a gesture and continued, "I am the one man in the world who can produce them exactly as you have written them." This sentence seemed to strike a responsive chord in Shaw and he listened to Pascal as he talked for an hour, convincing Shaw that he could do justice to his plays through the medium of motion pictures.

At the end of that hour, Shaw signed an agreement giving Pascal the rights to produce all of his stage plays as motion pictures. That contract was the beginning of a multimillion-dollar fortune for Pascal. Armed with this document, Pascal went to Hollywood and immediately won a contract with one of the biggest studios to produce all of Shaw's plays.

3. Program into your higher psychic mind centers a master motive to inspire you to great actions. If you are highly inspired in life, your dreams will reflect beauty, order, harmony, and happiness. However, if your conscious mind is filled with chaos, if you are disorderly in your person or environment, if you are living in confusion, discord, and friction, it is likely that your psychic mind centers have been programmed with negative forces that give your dreams an element of confusion and chaos.

DREAMS THAT REVEAL YOUR FEARS, ANXIETIES, AND WORRIES

You can check your own dreams to see if you are living under the whiplash of fear, worry, and anxiety. If so, you will see some of the following symbols in your dreams.

Do you often dream you are searching for something valuable but cannot find it? Do you start to go somewhere and then discover that you are not adequately dressed or cannot find the clothes you need? Sometimes in such dreams of disorientation you may find yourself wearing nothing and being embarrassed at the stares of those around you.

Do you sometimes dream that you are trying to catch a train or plane, and after many delays and setbacks, you finally arrive at the station only to find that the vehicle has left without you? This type of dream often means that you are not mentally prepared for your success and have, so to speak, missed the boat.

Such dreams of low motivation for achieving your goal may reveal you in situations where you lose your money, either accidentally or through gambling ventures. No matter how hard you try, you keep on losing money.

Sometimes these dreams will disguise themselves as policemen, judges, public officials, or political leaders. Contacts with them, in these confused dreams, usually lead to terrible problems and subsequent disasters. One man kept dreaming that he was drunk and driving a car. He was apprehended by a policeman who took him before a judge, and the judge sentenced him to a year in jail. This man neither drank nor drove recklessly in real life, but his psychic twin used these symbols to show that he was imprisoned by his present job and life circumstances, which represented his failure to achieve his life goals.

Sometimes these dreams will portray Hell with the flames burning the damned, and the dreamer tries to escape his punishment but cannot. Such a nightmare usually causes a person to awaken puzzled as to the meaning of his dream. It usually indicates conscience pangs of guilt because he has not achieved the goals he set for himself and remains in a Hell-like situation of poverty, lack, and limitation.

REGIMEN TO CHANGE YOUR DREAMS FOR THE BETTER

If you want to change the nature of your dreams from failure to success, from misery to happiness, and from suffering to enjoyment of life, change your psychic motivation. Remember, it is your psychic twin that causes you to dream. Call this psychic twin the psyche, subconscious, unconscious, or superconscious mind, it is all the same. Actually it is that intuitive side of your mind that knows how to demonstrate for you whatever pattern of events you consciously or unconsciously choose towards the destiny you are creating.

4. Program one or more of the following eight master motives into your psychic centers and then repeat or review these master motives every day of your life, to see if you are utilizing them in shaping your destiny.

(1) The desire for great achievement
(2) The desire to help your family
(3) The desire to improve yourself
(4) The desire to accumulate a fortune
(5) The desire for more knowledge and intellectual power
(6) The desire to have friends and a congenial social life
(7) The desire to be healthy and live a long life
(8) The desire to love and be loved

5. When you have formulated the particular master motives that are to be programmed into your higher psychic mind centers, you can begin to work each day to make them a living reality. You can have all eight motivations in your psychic drive for fulfillment of your dreams, or you may settle for only two or three; say you select the desire to accumulate a fortune, the desire to be healthy and live a long life, and the desire to love and be loved. You can work on these three first in order of their importance to you. Then add the other master motives as you require them.

6. Many people have one big master motive in life—to become rich. It is good to want riches, but it should not be the magnificent obsession of your life, for in so doing you are apt to lose out on the other great values that give life purpose and meaning.

A Gangster's Money Bought Everything but Peace, Health, and Love

I recall once being in a barber shop across the street from Carnegie Hall, where I had my lectures and studio, when a flashily dressed, heavyset man came bustling in with an air of great importance. He wore an expensive diamond ring on his finger and horseshoe-shaped diamond stickpin in his tie. Everyone dropped what they were doing to wait on him. When he left, the barber working on me said, "You know who that is, don't you?"

I confessed I didn't, and he told me, "That's a big underworld character who controls nightclubs that cater to mobsters, beer trucks, produce, and other legitimate and illegitimate businesses. He's worth millions and spends his money like water. But with all his fortune, he is suffering from heart trouble and high blood pressure that are killing him; last month his wife ran off with another man; he has been indicted by a federal grand jury on fraud charges that may land him in the penitentiary; his son was killed by a truck last year. Yes, you guessed it—a beer truck! His money can buy him everything but peace of mind, health, happiness, security, love, and Heaven."

Whenever you put your financial and material treasures above other values in life, remember that story. It is better to program yourself first with those enduring values of life than to set too high a goal for money.

Lao-tze and His Dream

The great Chinese poet and mystic Lao-tze once told his students, "Last night I had a very vivid dream in which I was a beautiful golden-winged butterfly, flying from flower to flower and enjoying myself greatly. That life as a butterfly seemed so real that when I awakened and found myself a man lying in bed, I thought to myself: *Am I now a butterfly dreaming I am a man, or am I a man dreaming myself to be a butterfly?*"

The dream and the dreamer are inextricably bound together in the warp and woof of destiny and cannot be separated. When you program yourself with dreams of greatness, you will become great. If you program your psychic centers with dreams of vast riches, you will be intuitively guided to do the things that will make you wealthy. If you dream of great achievements, of having a superior mind, brilliant gifts, and talents, your higher psychic centers must be motivated into spontaneous action that will result in the building of your tapestry of dreams into a solid structure that will be your future destiny.

REVIEW OF POINTS IN CHAPTER EIGHT

1. Millionaires I interviewed told me their secrets for building a fortune; they had projected in their dream fantasies a master motive for wanting to become rich and successful that went beyond a desire to just make money.

2. Aristotle Onassis had early visions of the great success he was to achieve as a shipping magnate, and they inspired his early actions in building has vast financial empire.

3. As a poor boy in Scotland, Andrew Carnegie projected himself in his dreams to America, the land of opportunity, where he would one day become successful and wealthy.

4. Edison, Eli Whitney, Robert Fulton, and other inventors were inspired by early youthful dreams of goal achievement, fame, and fortune, which they converted into living reality.

5. You can use a dream formula to turn your dreams into reality. *Dream, dare, and do*—This formula has been behind most of the world's great achievements.

6. Cecil Rhodes, ill with tuberculosis, was given up to die, but his dream formula directed him to program his higher psychic centers with the determination to become healthy and to achieve riches and fame.

7. A great producer, Gabriel Pascal, used his dream motivations to get the rights to produce George Bernard Shaw's plays as motion pictures.

8. You can use master motives to push your psychic mind into the direction of fame, fortune, good health, and great achievement.

9. Some dreams and symbols indicate that you lack a master motive and are suffering under the whiplash of fear, worry, and anxiety.

10. You can change these dreams of frustration and failure into master motives for great achievement, a desire to help your family, to improve yourself, to accumulate a fortune, and to find love-happiness.

11. An underworld character made millions of dollars but suffered from severe illness, lost his wife and child, and found that his money bought him everything but peace, health, love, and true spiritual fulfillment.

9

DREAM AWAY YOUR PROBLEMS WITH PSYCHIC GUIDANCE

Your dream world is often the battleground in which your psychic twins carry out pitched battle for supremacy. If your negative twin wins out, your dreams will become infested with scenes of horror; you will die a thousand deaths, plagued by a never-ending array of gruesome characters and frightening events. Finally, if this destructive, animalistic twin wins out, it will set out to destroy you and involve you in a hopeless struggle against the awesome odds of life in which you will give up in crushing defeat.

THE TWO OPPOSING LIFE AND DREAM FORCES

There are always these two opposing sides to your dreams as well as to life: good opposing evil, health opposing sickness, life opposing death, success pitted against failure, hate trying to overcome love, riches struggling against the encroachments of poverty, God opposed to the devil.

Emerson said, "All nature is bisected by duality."

Even the Bible tells of this strange duality and the attempt of the forces of evil to subvert the forces of good and truth. The devil tempted Christ by taking him to a high mountain and promising him the world if he would fall down and worship him. Christ's injunction "Get thee behind me, Satan!" has stood as the ultimate symbol of man's higher spiritual nature triumphing over the lower, bestial, and diabolical forces that try to destroy us.

Monsters like Adolf Hitler and Charles Manson are the soul's residue of evil and ultimate corruption when the dream of good is trampled into the mortal dust of lust, animalism, and hatred. Battlefields spring up, and prisons become filled with erring mortals; insane asylums attest to the fact that these conflicting sides of man's dream nature often put him in straitjackets and padded cells when he does not conform to the ideals and edicts of a power higher than his own.

In order to dream away your problems and let your higher psychic mind solve them while you sleep, you should know a little about the automatic mechanism of your subconscious. It is believed that this subconscious, or unconscious, is always working even while you sleep.

The subconscious frames your dreams and projects them into your consciousness in symbols of dramatic vividness. This subconscious is very much like a child in its simplicity and it will do anything that it is programmed to do, even to committing murder if the brain has been so conditioned.

Psychic Brainwashing Led to Mass Murder

An example of this type of so-called brainwashing occurred in the Manson case, where a group of young girls were masterminded by Manson into committing brutal and senseless murders. They even confessed to believing that Manson was the new Christ, sent to save suffering humanity from its sins. To their warped minds there was no crime in committing murder if in so doing they could achieve their objective of world peace for humanity. After all, their subconscious argued, if hundreds of thousands of human beings could be killed in the Vietnam War and millions killed in World War II, what would the lives of a few human guinea pigs matter in the long course of history? The devil part of their psychic twins won out and these innocent-looking girls committed crimes of such brutality that hardened detectives admitted they were sick when they viewed the bodies of persons the girls butchered in cold blood.

PROGRAM YOUR PSYCHIC CENTERS WITH POSITIVE FORCES

You can program these psychic mind centers with all the positive forces of life, and they will set to work while you sleep, solving problems, showing you how to obtain needed money, giving you information to help you find a job. These higher psychic mind centers know your mental and physical potentials; they will always work within the range of your own capabilities.

You may program this higher self with the thought you want a million dollars quickly and be very disappointed to find out that there is no response from this higher psychic mind. The reason for this is the fact that your psychic twin knows the unreasonableness of this request. You may not be worth a million dollars in your present capacity and training. However, you can reasonably ask for smaller sums and be guided to getting them if you have trained yourself in some specific way or have a trade or occupation that has prepared you for earning more.

A Young Man Projected a Vast Fortune in His Dreams

A young man once dreamed that he was the head of a large organization manufacturing some product for the home. In his dream he made millions of dollars and spent it lavishly. He had this dream over and over, but not being versed in the science of dreamology, he did not know what it was trying to tell him.

When this young man married at the age of twenty-four, he was working for someone else, but on his honeymoon he gave his wife an undated check for $25,000 and told her that he could not afford to buy her a wedding gift such as an expensive piece of jewelry, but that she was to keep this check in a safe place and at the end of ten years, on their anniversary, she was to cash it.

Shortly after his wedding, this young man got into the then relatively new plastics industry. He forged ahead and soon had his own small manufacturing plant in Los Angeles. In exactly ten years from that time he was one of the leading manufacturers in the plastics industry. He had already forgotten about the $25,000 check he had given to his wife, but on their tenth wedding anniversary his wife confidently dated the check, presented it at the bank, and it was paid! This man's psychic twin had never forgotten his commitment to that debt, and it paid off by pushing him into the one business where he could become a millionaire within ten years.

REGIMEN TO DREAM AWAY YOUR PROBLEMS

1. There is a problem-solving side to your consciousness, just as there is a problem-making side. The solution to your problems is contained within the problems themselves. Your higher psychic twin is aware of this, and it is always searching for the solutions to vexing problems that arise in your life. It is very much like a computer that has been programmed with all kinds of information. In fact, no computer, no matter how carefully it is manufactured, can ever produce more than is programmed within its mechanical brain.

You can feed data into your subconscious higher mind, and it will carefully sort out all the information you send it and file it away in neat little compartments that are labeled for future use. Your subconscious then receives the nerve impulses from your conscious mind that send it scurrying to these various compartments to search for the best possible combination of facts to fit that particular problem.

Next your subconscious will put together all the answers to your questions and show you all the possible solutions to your problems. It will then put them into your dreams, in symbolical form, giving you clues as to what you should do to solve the problems.

In these subconscious compartments of your brain there are labels that say, "ways to make more money," "romantic problems," "how to keep the body healthy," "creative ideas for success," "potential gifts and talents," "formulas and inventions," "songs, stories and art," and "human realtionships."

2. Whenever you have a problem and want your psychic twin to help you solve it, you must go into a dreamlike state called meditation and focus your conscious mind on the problem itself. Then with your eyes closed, you simply give the problem to your subconscious twin in thoughts or words that can be like this:

I have a problem. I want to change my work and have a job with more money and less effort that fits my talents. Show me how I can find such a job and improve my financial position.

3. After you have stated your problem and sat for about five minutes in silence, you can get up and go about your regular affairs and not worry about it any longer. Do this two or three times a day, especially at night, just before going to sleep. Repeat the problem, ask for its solution, and drift off to sleep, knowing that while you sleep, your psychic twin is going to get busy examining all your subconscious files to see what information stored there can be drawn upon to help you solve your problem.

Putting Down Empty Buckets into Empty Wells

Now if your mental bins are empty, and you have put nothing into your subconscious in the way of education, training in some specific occupation, or other information that could help you obtain a better position, obviously your psychic twin will have to devise a new method for you to achieve your goal of a job change for more money or advancement in your work. However, this psychic twin is very ingenious and sometimes can take nothing and make it into something, projecting onto your psychic screen some new combination of latent talents you possess that could make you a success.

Someone once said of a failure, "He spent his entire youth letting empty buckets down into empty wells and now he is spending his old age pulling them up again, empty."

This is true about your subconscious twin; you must have the materials there for it to do its best work. Then it will get busy showing you how to use those talents and that information to your best advantage.

This Woman's Dreams Led Her to a Prosperous Business

A woman who had been left a widow with very little money other than a gas pump in the middle of a western desert had a great desire to increase her income, but there seemed to be no way out of her financial dilemma. Because a new highway had been built that bypassed her gas station, she was on a side road where very few cars passed. She frantically sought help from her subconscious, without knowing she was tapping this power, by asking herself, "Now what shall I do? I have no way to get more money. No one will buy this worthless property, and my insurance money is getting awfully low. Help me, God, to find a solution!"

A few nights later this woman had a very puzzling dream. She was lost in a barren, desert area, very much like the one where she lived. She was searching for a road or some signs of habitation but could find none. She found herself suddenly in an area where there were dense growths of cactus plants, towering like monsters around her. As she stumbled through this cactus forest, she felt suffocated and fell to the ground, suffering from thirst and exhaustion.

Then she remembered hearing that cactus plants stored water so that many a prospector who had been lost in the desert lived for days on water from the cactus. She broke down a stem of a large cactus and out flowed cool, delicious water. She slaked her thirst and had the strength to get up and struggle towards a road that led to a fabulous city on a hill that glistened like gold. Then she awoke from her dream, and her mouth seemed as parched with thirst as it had been in her dream.

For several days, she puzzled over the meaning of that dream, still sending out her distress call to her subconscious (which in her case she called "God"). She felt the dream she had was trying in some way to give her a message, but she could not decipher that message.

This woman's psychic twin had heard her distress call and had set to work to discover some method to increase her income in that desert area where there was nothing but sand and wild cactus.

In the empty weeks ahead, she looked around for something to do. She discovered many different species of cactus growing wild in her back yard, some with beautiful purple and crimson flowers on them. She had some pots lying around, so she planted cactus shoots in them and created a little garden area around her gas station. Soon she had dozens of little plants growing in small pots, and they made a very attractive natural decoration in front of her gas station.

One day a car pulled up to the station. The driver admitted that he was lost, having strayed from the main highway, and asked for directions for getting back onto the road. He looked at the large display of miniature cactus plants and evinced an interest in them. On learning that this was the woman's hobby, he said, "I think there would be a big market for these miniature cactus plants in Los Angeles. I have a big nursery on the outskirts of the city and I supply many big florists. How about furnishing me with some of these cactus plants? I think I can find a good outlet for them."

They worked out a deal, and the man drove off with a few samples in his car. The result of this accidental meeting was phenomenal; the man continued to buy large quantities of cactus plants, and soon the woman had a flourishing business, making her more money a year than the gas station had ever made!

The Bible asks, "What hast thou in thine house?" When you ask your psychic twin to reveal methods for solving your problems you are literally undertaking a subconscious search of all the compartments in your unconscious mind where facts may be stored that can help you find a solution to your problems.

FINANCIAL AND BUSINESS PROBLEMS

Sit each day for a few moments, at least three times a day, and ask your psychic twin how you can get more money. Mentally go over all the potentials for increasing your income, the objects you could sell, the loans you might make, the property you have and how it could be used as collateral for a loan. It is necessary for you to examine consciously all the known means for increasing your income in order for your psychic twin to be motivated by your inner desires and needs. If it is being programmed each day by your conscious desire to have more money, it will soon set to work and bring you some ideas that can make more money for you.

A Man Had Dreams of Finding Money and Found $200

To show how this method works, a man had a frequent dream that he found sums of money on the street or in strange places.

He would pick up ten- and twenty-dollar bills and sometimes bigger denominations. When he awoke, he tried to figure out what his dreams were trying to tell him.

One day something made him go into a secondhand furniture store to buy a chest of drawers he needed for a bedroom. He found one that seemed to be just what he needed, so he put it into the trunk of his car and took it home. His wife decided to clean the drawers before using the chest, and as she pulled up the paper that was in the top drawer, she found ten twenty-dollar bills hidden under the paper!

Could the subconscious have the ability to go out while we sleep and explore the astral realms, like mystics believe, and discover sources of hidden money, oil wells, goldmines, or other valuables? Dr. Joseph B. Rhine of Duke University came to the conclusion after years of research in extrasensory perception that something more than the mind was involved in mental telepathy, psychic phenomena, and precognition, something akin to a soul or spirit in man that could project its intelligence to other realms while the person slept, revealing secrets of the universe not known to the ordinary five senses.

$15,000 Came to This Woman through a Dream

A woman had recurring dreams in which she found money while walking down the street. She also dreamed that money came to her in strange and unusual ways, and she kept trying to make these dreams come true by buying lottery tickets and entering all kinds of contests, but she never won anything.

Then one day her bathroom drain became clogged and she had to call in a plumber. When he took the plumbing apart, he found a large wad of green paper stuck in the drain. Upon closer examination it turned out to be money! The woman dried out the bills, which were in large denominations, and they were still intact and identifiable. They amounted to $15,000! She called the police, who checked the bills carefully to see if they were marked or counterfeit. They were genuine, and as no one came to claim the money within the legal time limit, this woman kept that large sum of money!

ROMANTIC AND MARITAL PROBLEMS

If you are having some romantic or marital problem and need guidance to solve it, use the method given above. Sit quietly in meditation, and program your psychic twin with the problem, clearly stating all sides of it in detail. Then go to sleep, confident that the solution will come to you while you are sleeping. It will masquerade as a symbol or dream, which you should examine carefully to find its exact meaning.

You may dream of consulting a lawyer to get a divorce, and the dream may be accompanied by great grief as you weep and feel that you have lost something precious. This could certainly be an indication that your subconscious twin is trying to tell you to forget seeing a lawyer and getting the divorce, as it will break your heart. It may be trying to tell you to find another solution to your problems of incompatibility. However, if you feel lighthearted in the dream, or see yourself being freed of chains, or being let out of prison, you may be receiving a message from your psychic twin saying, in effect, "Go ahead, get the divorce. Take off the chains that have bound you all these years, get out of the prison that holds you back, and be free!"

If your dreams are filled with suppressed longings and you find yourself going from one love to another, always searching for fulfillment, this could be a clue that you had better settle down, marry, have a family, and end your hunt for the perfect soul mate.

If a woman dreams of having a child out of wedlock and anxiously searches for the father but cannot find him, this could be a clue that her psychic twin is trying to tell her to be cautious in her relationships with men, to avoid pregnancy, or not to trust some man who may be eager to marry her.

PROBLEMS WITH RELATIVES AND COWORKERS

Problems dealing with human relationships are frequent. Often a person will be in a continual state of turmoil because he does not get along with his coworkers, has run-ins with his in-laws, and his landlord causes him difficulty.

How can one solve such problems? Review your relationships with various people in your life, especially just before you drop off to sleep. Then activate dream-dramas in which you consciously project yourself into various situations with these people and ask your psychic twin to give you the solution to these problems while you sleep. You might pose the hypothetical question: "What would I do if confronted with this situation in my life?" Then review the various problems that have arisen or might arise, and give your psychic twin the elements of the drama you wish resolved. You probably will have vivid dreams in which you and your antagonist are pitted against each other in furious battle; one of you will be victorious, or it will end in your destroying your enemy, and you will feel a deep sense of relief that you are rid of the person.

He Dreamed of Killing His Mother-in-law

One man let his mother-in-law move in shortly after marriage, as she was a widow and had no place else to go. He resented the mother-in-law, as she interfered and seemed to be intent on breaking up his marriage.

Every night, before drifting off to sleep, he would spend time thinking up ways of getting rid of the troublesome woman. He conceived all kinds of subtle plots, including poisoning her, or killing her in some other manner and then getting rid of the body.

His dreams became haunted with leering faces of witches and monsters who were always hovering over him, cackling, and trying to destroy him. He would fight these phantoms in his dreams, but they always seemed to win. Sometimes he dreamed that he was killing his mother-in-law and then found that he had no way of disposing of the body. The police would come and take him to jail. Once he dreamed that he buried the body in the basement, but the police found the shallow grave and arrested him for murder.

This man finally developed a severe case of bleeding stomach ulcers and went for tests and examinations to determine the cause. The doctor placed him under a fluoroscope, which showed his stomach in action trying to digest the barium he had been fed for the purpose. A word association test was given him of innocent words like house, dog, and water and there was no reaction. But when the doctor said "mother-in-law" the man's stomach jumped as though it had been shot. The doctor asked, "Have you been having mother-in-law trouble lately?"

The man admitted he had wanted to kill the interfering woman. Then the doctor told him that his ulcers were a direct result of suppressed hatred and rage. Instead of killing his mother-in-law, the man was actually killing himself.

Upon the doctor's advice the couple moved the mother-in-law out of the house. The man's nightmares of killing suddenly ended, and his ulcers healed completely.

REVIEW OF POINTS IN CHAPTER NINE

1. Your dream world often becomes the battleground in which each of your psychic twins tries to gain supremacy, causing dreams that are often nightmares of terror.
2. The subconscious works to project into your consciousness strange symbols and vivid pictures of these conflicts between evil and good.
3. Hitler used brainwashing techniques as did mass murderer Charles Manson.
4. You can program your higher psychic mind centers with all the positive forces of health, life, good, riches, and happiness, so you will be shown how to achieve the perfect life.
5. A young man used his dream consciousness to put him into the plastics industry. In ten years he had become a multimillionaire.
6. There is a side of your subconscious that creates your problems and a side that solves them; you can use the latter to help you overcome life's problems.
7. The subconscious is like a computer, which can be programmed by putting into the higher psychic centers the information for solving problems.
8. The various compartments in your subconscious are la-

beled with every known type of information, from ways to make more money to solving problems in human relationships.

9. A widow who had a money problem received from her subconscious a secret for making money that made her financially independent.

10. You can solve your financial and business problems by using this method of psychic programming.

11. A man bought a secondhand chest and found $200 concealed in one of its drawers. He had programmed himself with dreams that he would find money.

12. You can solve your romantic and marital problems by using your psychic twin to release the solutions to your problems in dreams.

13. You can solve problems of human relationships by programming your dream-self with solutions.

10

CLAIRVOYANT DREAMS TO PROTECT YOU FROM SICKNESS, ACCIDENT, AND TRAGEDY

In recent studies of ESP and related subjects, scientists have found that the human mind does not recognize the barriers of manmade time and space. As Einstein proved, in the realm of the infinite there are no such barriers. These scientists now feel that the higher psychic centers of the human brain are able to overcome these barriers of time and to project dreams and clairvoyant visions not only of the past but also of future events.

Scientists have proven ESP and mental telepathy by having a person send mental messages for a distance of a thousand miles to a subject who accurately received the messages.

Twins Projected Thoughts to Each Other

A set of twins was separated a distance of 300 miles, and one was urged to think certain thoughts in order to accelerate his breathing and pulse beat, and the other twin, attached to a brain-measuring machine 300 miles away, went through the same physiological responses, even though he did not know what his twin brother was thinking or doing. His heartbeat increased at the same moment his brother's did, and his blood pressure even went up at the identical moment.

A Queen Who Dreamed of Her Son's Downfall

I once met Queen Mother Nazli of Egypt when I was doing a book on the story of her life. She was the mother of King Farouk. When he ascended the throne at the age of eighteen, he was a very handsome and persuasive youngster whom everyone loved. However, over the years, sycophants around him influenced him and turned him into an egotistical glutton who dissipated the wealth of his country on drunken feasts and orgies.

One night his mother had a psychic dream in which she saw angry crowds storming their palace at Alexandria and setting it afire. She went to King Farouk and begged him to flee, but he was in such a drunken stupor that he could not be roused from his bed. As she fled from the burning palace, she looked back and saw it crumbling into smoldering ruins, with her son buried beneath the rubble.

This frightening nightmare caused the Queen to pack her belongings and leave the country. She went to France, where she remained for some months. Then came the tragic news that mobs had indeed stormed the palace, that there had been a revolution in Egypt, and that King Farouk had been given a chance to escape with his life.

Queen Nazli did not have to be a dream expert to interpret her clairvoyant dream. Its images of the destruction of the palace, symbol of Farouk's power, and his being trapped in the ruins were prophetic in the sense that he was stripped of all power before being permitted to leave his country.

SOME CLAIRVOYANT DREAMS AND WHAT THEY MEAN

As dreams frequently masquerade in forms different from reality, one must constantly be aware of these hidden meanings. Sometimes a nightmare will include wild animals trying to catch one, and the dreamer wakes up in terror.

Such a dream may in no way relate to actual physical danger, as in our society wild animals are seldom loose. But it can relate to psychological states of consciousness. The person may be living an emotionally suppressed life in which the animals of passion, aggression, and conquest have been forcibly stilled because of the mores of society or religion.

Thus it was no surprise to me in our dream laboratory to hear a mild-mannered spinster of forty-five tell that in her dreams she had been pursued by wild animals like lions and tigers and that she awakened from these horrible nightmares in a cold sweat. Upon analyzing her dreams, we came to the conclusion that the wild animals were in reality her own lusts and sexual appetites that could be unleashed safely only in her dreams. What her psychic twin was trying to tell her in these dreams was very simple: "Look, get out and live, love and be wild for a change. If you never cut loose and do the things that give animal satisfaction and enjoyment, you will wither on the vine of life and die without ever being a complete and fulfilled human being."

However, the same clairvoyant vision may come to another type of person, who is engaging in sexual promiscuity. It can also relate to overeating and overdrinking—burning the candle at both ends, so to speak. The dream may be warning of coming illness, as uncontrolled appetites lead to physical and mental deterioration. What the psychic twin is trying to say in this case would be: "Slow down a little. You're letting your appetites (the wild animals) get control of your life, and soon they will destroy you with bad health, high blood pressure, heart trouble, and other ailments."

Dreams in which fire plays an important part are significant, sometimes as symbolizing something of a destructive nature that may happen. But fire may also represent a purifying element, burning away the old, past life and bringing new life and regeneration.

Recurring dreams of fire may also prophesy loss. Such dreams might include being trapped in flames, or having one's home burned, or losing valuable objects or papers through fire. The dream does not always mean that the losses will occur through fire; they might occur through theft or accident. The psychic twin uses dreams of fire to designate many various forms of disaster.

A Dream of Fire Warned of a Husband's Infidelity

One woman in our dream laboratory told of a persistent dream in which her home was burning. She was in an upstairs bedroom and had no way of escaping the flames. She went to the windows but found they would not open, and she could not jump, as it was too great a distance. Finally the floor collapsed under her, sending her tumbling into the flaming ruins. She then awoke in terror.

Upon analysis, we found that the dream of fire did not relate to actual danger from flames. She had been married to one man for twenty years, only to find that he was now having an affair with another woman and wanted a divorce so that he could marry his mistress. The wife was being given the clairvoyant vision of her home being destroyed by flames to symbolize the flames of her husband's passion for someone else. She decided to act upon this interpretation of her dream to avoid being destroyed by her husband's infidelity. She changed her attitude towards him, having a frank discussion, in which she promised to forgive him for his escapade if he would promise to stop seeing the other woman. They worked out their problems amicably, and her marriage was saved from ruin.

Their Homes Were Saved by Dreams of Fire

One woman had recurring dreams of fires that sometimes destroyed her home and sometimes objects she valued. She took the dreams literally, believing that they were trying to warn her of danger of a real fire destroying her home. She and her husband had recently converted their basement into a playroom for their three teenaged children. In the process they had taken some kind of beaverboard to cover the ceiling where rafters and electrical wiring were concealed.

She called in an electrician to examine this room to see if perhaps they had overlooked some danger. The man found that there were loose wires in back of the highly inflammable beaverboard that could have set fire to the house while they slept. He advised them to change the wiring and to use a fireproof type of material for the ceiling, thus averting what was a very real danger of a tragic fire.

Another woman who told us her dreams in our laboratory said she kept dreaming of fires, so she made up her mind that something was trying to come through as a warning. Since she had no fire extinguishers in the house, she and her husband went out and bought three, one for the kitchen and two for the bedrooms. Two weeks later, fat ignited in her oven. When she opened the oven door, the flames set fire to the nearby wall, and she was able to put them out with her fire extinguisher!

REGIMEN FOR DEVELOPING CLAIRVOYANT DREAM POWER

1. To sensitize your higher psychic and clairvoyant mind centers so that through your dreams they can guide you and protect you, sit every day and program these higher psychic centers with visual images that you consciously choose.

Make these visual images, sometimes called daydreams, as real as possible. Choose only positive projections, not negative ones. The entire purpose of this type of clairvoyant exercise is to give your psychic mind visual images that you will readily recognize if in your dreams they are trying to warn you or guide you to some course of action in your everyday life.

Take, for example, the psychic projection that you are on an airplane, going on a vacation to some foreign country. In your daydream see yourself on the airplane; see the country you are going to. If you need visual aids, get travel literature and carefully choose the places you wish to visit. Then in your daydreams project yourself to those places.

When your higher psychic mind receives these mental impulses, it will carefully store them away in your subconscious compartments and bring about the means for your taking such trips in the future, and it will also warn you if there is any danger on the journey.

A Dream of Accident Foretold Disaster

I recall an incident in which a prominent woman, who was the head of a large perfume company, had a very vivid dream before she and her husband were to take a trip to Europe one summer. She saw written in letters of flame on her living room wall the warning "Do not take this trip; there will be great danger." In her dream the letters of this message kept flashing on and off like a neon sign. When she awoke she felt a very disquieting sense of some kind of tragedy. She talked it over with her husband and told him she felt something tragic would happen on the trip and that they should cancel it. However, he wanted to go so he convinced her that it was only a dream and meant nothing. They took the trip, and just as her clairvoyant dream had suggested, she had an accident that crippled her for the remainder of her life!

2. For psychic and clairvoyant guidance in your own life, project mental images of various types of situations that might occur. Review these realistically, seeing all sides of the problem and then giving it to your psychic twin to solve. This can be a problem relating to love or marriage, or it can be a situation in which you are not able to find your true soul mate and you ask for guidance of your higher psychic mind. The higher mind within you will store this information in its files, drawing on it to warn you in clairvoyant dreams of dangers or disturbances that you may face in the romantic part of your life.

Her Dream Warned of Impending Divorce

One woman in our dream laboratory told of frequent dreams of her swimming in deep water, that she was getting along fine when she suddenly found that something was wrong and she was sinking. She became panicky and thought that it might be a riptide. She had heard that if caught in such a tide one simply turned over and floated until it had spent itself. She tried doing this but couldn't get onto her back; she was sinking in the water and finally gave up in despair and felt she was drowning. She awoke with a feeling of suffocation and could not go back to sleep for some time, wondering what the dream could possibly mean.

In analyzing the dream she told us that she had been married for five years to a wonderful man, but lately she had found someone else that she loved more than her husband. In those years with her husband she had never found complete sexual fulfillment; he was cold and distant and lacked the ability to arouse her fully. When she met this other man, he was everything she had ever dreamed of in a lover. She had a secret romance with him, and it had gone on for some time. Now she felt it was time to let her husband know she wanted a divorce.

Of course, any dreams of water generally relate to the hidden or submerged sexual nature. The woman's feeling of drowning indicated that her marriage was failing. A riptide could symbolize a sudden calamity in the department of love or marriage and cautions you not to enter into a romantic alliance with a person who might "pull you under." However, dreams about water can also relate to the regenerative process of dying and being reborn. There are the waters of baptism, in which a person becomes spiritually reborn. Water also relates to birth, when the sac surrounding the baby breaks and lets the water escape. This woman was being told by her psychic twin that, in dying to the old love or marriage, she was being reborn in the new sexual relationship that gave her renewed life and feelings.

3. If you wish to receive clairvoyant guidance to protect you from various forms of danger, such as muggings, accidents in cars, planes, or boats, fire, falling under a vehicle or down a flight of stairs, you can review consciously the various things that might happen to you in life and ask your higher psychic twin to protect you and guide you in life so you can avoid such dangers.

DREAM SYMBOLS THAT WARN OF DANGER

You might receive any one of a number of various symbols indicating these warnings against danger. Seeing in a dream an unknown assailant armed with a knife, gun, or other weapon could indicate possible danger of being assaulted in your home or on the street. It could also be a psychic warning of hidden dangers, treachery, or deceit from someone you know.

A Dream Warned Him That His Partner Was Stealing from Him

One man reported in our dream analysis sessions that he had dreamed several times that someone had broken into his shop, and when he arrived there in the morning he was confronted by a gunman who demanded that he open the safe and give him his money.

Of course, the first interpretation of such a psychic dream would be that this man had consciously reviewed this possibility so often in his consciousness that it was a vivid playback of his psychic mind, making it a realistic dream.

No such robbery from an armed assailant ever did happen to this man but a few weeks after having these dreams, he found out that his business partner was dipping into the till and robbing him of considerable cash! The dream side of his nature had somehow made this evaluation from the circumstances in his life and revealed the theft in this way.

She Dreamed of One Accident and Had Another

A middle-aged woman once told me of her dream that while she was skiing on steep slopes, she became entangled in her skis and fell, breaking both legs. As she had never skied in her life, she couldn't possibly imagine what her psychic twin was trying to warn her about. Two weeks after she had this dream, she was crossing her living room when she slipped on a rug, fell down, and broke her arm in two places!

Many people have warning dreams of danger, accidents, fires, and physical assaults, which clothe themselves in these strange ways. If you do have such a clairvoyant dream that keeps repeating itself, examine it carefully, not only for the obvious clues, but for the hidden, submerged meanings.

She Dreamed Her Child Was Drowning

Another woman who had a child at the crawling stage had vivid dreams in which the child was in danger of falling, drowning, being burned in fires, and various other tragedies. As a mother's protective instincts often cause her to mentally review all forms of danger that might befall her children, the subconscious often becomes saturated with dreams that may only represent a mother's natural concern. One day this woman accidentally left open the door of her patio, which led to the swimming pool outside. She was in the kitchen only a few moments while her child was playing on the living room floor. When she returned to the living room she saw that the child was gone. She then saw the open door leading to the pool, and rushing out to the patio, she found her baby floating, face down, in the pool! She screamed for help, and neighbors heard her and rushed to her aid. They pulled the child out and gave him mouth to mouth resuscitation, which brought him back to life. Sometimes, however, no matter what steps we take to heed our clairvoyant dreams of disaster, a moment of carelessness can cost a life.

REVIEW OF POINTS IN CHAPTER TEN

1. Scientists have found that ESP, precognition, and mental telepathy can exist in the dream states, just as they often do in the conscious, waking states.
2. Queen Mother Nazli of Egypt was warned by dreams of disaster for her son King Farouk that caused her to move out of Egypt before the disaster occurred.
3. Some clairvoyant dreams of danger and tragedy masquerade in strange ways.
4. A middle-aged spinster had dreams of wild animals that pursued her; these were analyzed to indicate that her psychic twin was trying to tell her to have some sexual experiences before she died.
5. Dreams of fires that destroy valuables or threaten life could mean danger from actual fires, but they more often indicate a marriage, a business, or some personal relationship that is being destroyed.
6. One woman dreamed of fire and saved her home when she had an electrician examine a playroom where he found defective wiring.
7. You can sensitize the higher psychic mind so that it can use dreams to guide you and protect you from various forms of danger.
8. A woman in a dream saw written in letters of flame these

words: "Do not take this trip; there will be great danger." She disobeyed the warning of her dream, and on the trip she had an accident that crippled her for life.

9. A dream of drowning or other dreams connected with water can be read literally as a warning to be cautious in swimming. Or it can be symbolical, indicating some sexual suppressions that may be destroying one's chances for romantic happiness.

10. Clairvoyant dreams of guns, knives, or other weapons can relate to actual dangers from burglars, rapists, or muggers, or they can symbolize treachery or deceit from people close to you. A man dreamed of armed robbery, only to find that his business partner was dipping into the till and taking large sums of money.

11. A woman kept dreaming that her young child was in danger. One day her child fell into a pool and nearly drowned.

11
HOW TO FASHION YOUR PERFECT LOVE LIFE THROUGH YOUR DREAMS

Everyone dreams of finding his perfect soul mate and, as the fairytale says, "living happily ever after." Unfortunately, this rosy prospect seldom materializes for most people, and they find themselves constantly frustrated, married to the wrong mate, or living a false life in which they masquerade as happy individuals when in reality their hearts are breaking.

Is there any way by which we may use dream therapy for finding happiness in love and marriage?

In recent laboratory studies, scientists have found that we are often influenced in fashioning the events of our lives through our dreams. This principle can work both ways: Our dreams are the direct results of our life experiences, good or bad; and, conversely, our lives are affected by our dreams.

The things that you put into your consciousness can, in effect, produce dreams that are symptomatic of the events of your life. If you are experiencing a wonderful relationship in love or marriage, and things are going smoothly, you will find that your dreams are filled with happy, bright events that reflect this romantic bliss.

But if you are having romantic or marital problems, you will probably have dreams that are troubled and filled with a never-ending series of disturbing complications. Some of these may mask themselves, for your subconscious seeks to conceal its messages.

A Fifteen-Year-Old Girl Dreamed of Sex with Her Brother-in-Law

A fifteen-year-old girl had recurring dreams in which her handsome young brother-in-law was making love to her, which frightened her but at the same time gave her pleasure. She had daytime fantasies that their love act was consummated, and one night she awoke to find that her brother-in-law was indeed carrying out her fantasy, even though his wife lay nearby in deep sleep! This relationship continued until the girl became pregnant, but she concealed the identity of the father, saying that he was one of her high school boyfriends, whose name she refused to give. Her sexual desires had communicated themselves to her psychic twin, who caused her to fulfill these desires through dreams. If they had ended as dream fantasies, no harm would have been done.

Just as you can solve your problems through your dreams or have great ideas for inventions, artistic creations, and business through projecting them into your dream consciousness, so, too, you may shape the events of your romantic life in your dreams and see them come into focus in reality.

REGIMEN FOR PROJECTING A PERFECT LOVE LIFE

1. If you are searching for your true soul mate, give your psychic twin the specifications for the type of person you want to love and marry. Since this psychic twin constantly gives you guidance in every other department of your life, is it not logical to suppose that it will be able to find the perfect soul mate?

A girl came to me after one of our dream laboratory sessions and said, "I am projecting tonight the perfect soul mate that I want to attract. He must be six feet tall, athletically built, have brown eyes, auburn hair, and be graduated from a leading university like Harvard, Yale, or Princeton." Then she paused a moment, rolled her eyes coquettishly, and asked, "Is that too much to expect of a millionaire?" I never did follow up this girl's dream projection of her true soul mate, but she was on the right track, although we cannot always be that specific in tracking down our dream lovers.

You can, however, mentally determine the mental qualities you desire in a soul mate. Tell your psychic twin to guide you in your dreams to finding someone who is kind, loving, considerate, loyal, and honest. The physical requirements are secondary. You can even mentally project the type of emotional expression he is to have, smiling, warm, and friendly, for example, rather than aloof, isolated, and sarcastic.

When you have programmed the perfect dream lover into your psychic mind, you will soon begin to have dreams that bring this mythical lover into focus. Some of the symbols that your love-dreams may clothe themselves in are as follows:

You may have visions of yourself at the altar, waiting to be married. Or you may see a fleeting glimpse of the loved one at a party and project a desire to meet him. You may dream of wedding gowns, wedding cakes, churches with lighted candles, or see yourself on your honeymoon with your dream lover.

2. After you have identified yourself with your mythical dream lover, put yourself into situations where you might meet people who measure up to your dream fantasies. If you have projected to your psychic twin the image of meeting a lover who is highly sophisticated, well educated, and a success in business, you certainly would not find him in an environment frequented by hippies, drug addicts, or alcoholics. You would find him in a smart café, a respectable home, or a church gathering.

Her Dream of a Hawaiian Honeymoon Came True

One young woman who projected meeting her true soul mate had frequent dreams that she was on a plane flying to Hawaii. As she lived in California, this was not an unlikely possibility, and she felt an urge to go there on her vacation. Finally, she yielded to this desire and went on the trip. She carefully looked over the plane to see if there was any sign of her dream lover there, but found only middle-aged schoolteachers, older businessmen, and a few single girls.

She checked in at her hotel on the beach at Waikiki, and she had breakfast each morning out in the beautiful courtyard facing the ocean. On the third day after her arrival, while she was breakfasting alone, a young man asked her if he might sit with her, as the other tables were filled. She looked up at a tall, handsome young man who was smiling pleasantly, and she found herself thinking, *Why, this is the man of my dreams!* He sat down, and soon they were chatting as familiarly as though they had known each other a lifetime. Her soul mate had gravitated to her in Hawaii, that distant land of beauty and romance. He happened to live in San Francisco, the same city she did. They fell in love with each other, and soon after returning home, they were married.

3. Give your psychic twin suggestions that will help it decide exactly how you should attract your true soul mate. These suggestions can be patterned in this way, or you may make up your own:

I desire fulfillment in love and marriage. I want to attract a mate who will like the same things I do; one who is kind, loving, and considerate. I want to be guided to finding this soul mate. Give me instructions as to how to find my mate, where to go, what to do, and how I will know if it is the right person for me.

Repeat this suggestion each night just before going to sleep. Keep thinking the thoughts embodied in the words, see the fulfillment of that desire, and drop off to sleep, asking your psychic twin to give you dreams that will bring your soul mate into the picture.

4. If you have been experiencing difficulties in love and marriage, you are probably having dreams that reflect confusion, disorientation, and frustration. Check your dreams carefully to see if this is the case; then try to analyze them in the light of your daily experiences in the departments of love and marriage.

Such troubled dreams may include symbols of your frustration, such as obstacles placed in your path when you're trying to reach your goal. Or in your dreams you may find yourself experiencing legal difficulties, never being able to get together with the lawyer or other people involved. Sometimes you may dream of others who are acting together to defeat and confuse you. These are all symbols of your own romantic frustrations and will no doubt exist as long as that life situation exists. To change the nature of your dreams from unpleasant to pleasant, it is necessary that you change your life situations drastically.

5. You can also program your psychic self with visual images of the perfect romance you wish to attain. Everyone has dream fantasies in which one visualizes the ideal lover and goes through various romantic acts with that person. If these romantic fantasies follow you into your dream world, you can be sure that your psychic twin is trying to tell you, "Go ahead! Follow your dream fantasies in real life, it will be o.k. with me."

Her Dream of Wife Swapping Came True

One case of sexual dream fantasies that led to true life fulfillment came to light in our dream laboratory sessions. A married woman admitted that she had recently been having dreams of sexual activity with men other than her husband. In one such dream that occured frequently, she found herself at a private home where a big party was underway. When the guests entered, each was told to disrobe and given a sheet to cover his body. Sometime later in the party, the guests began to drop their sheets and started to pair off with other guests. She tried to find her husband but the similarity of all the guests with their sheets confused her, and she finally found herself being taken over by another man who engaged her in sexual activity. She stopped worrying about finding her husband and gave herself with abandon to the new lover. Then she looked at the couple lying next to them and saw that it was her husband making love to a strange girl. She wasn't shocked, as she noticed what pleasure it gave him. When she awakened from this confusing dream, she could not understand its meaning until it was analyzed in the dream laboratory.

The first and most obvious meaning of the dream was that this woman, after five years of marriage, had become bored with her marriage and with her husband's lovemaking. Subconsciously, she longed for a new mate, but her training had been religious and conventional, and she could not face getting a divorce or seeking out other romantic partners. So her dream world became peopled with fantasies in which she could act out her own suppressed desires.

After this dream had been analyzed the woman began to have fewer such dream-fantasies, for now that she knew the nature of the dream it no longer troubled her. However, sometime later, her husband came to her and said, "We've been invited to a party tomorrow night that might be fun." He then proceeded to tell her that young couples like themselves would be there, and it would amount to a wife-swapping type of thing—would she be interested in going? Now that her husband had broached the subject, all mental barriers were down; she went to the party and relived the experiences of her dream-fantasies. She and her husband were happier than they had ever been in this new experience that gave them both such pleasure, and all thoughts of divorce were abandoned. Obviously, such emotional experiences should be avoided by those who are happy in their marriages, and should be engaged in only by those who have no hang-ups about sexual promiscuity.

6. Every young person begins to build the pattern for his future love life in the adolescent years. These youthful ideals about love and marriage are usually patterned after the lives of their parents, who are the closest models they have to copy.

If the parents lived in an atmosphere of love and consideration, showing love for their children and respect for each other, the children normally reflect these patterns in their own adult lives.

If there has been an atmosphere of bickering and lack of love in the home, the children may become quarrelsome and carry over this pattern into their own marriages.

Children from Broken Homes Have Troubled Dreams

Statistics show that children who come from broken homes usually wind up having more than one marriage. It is obvious that you can set the stage for romantic happiness for your own children by showing affection for them as well as for your mate. Children from broken homes have troubled dreams in which they are searching for something they cannot find; or they find themselves in a long tunnel, trying to get out and never succeeding. Many of their dreams show them lost in a dark forest with frightening phantoms on all sides trying to catch them. In the dreams they run in terror, and they awaken screaming.

If your childhood was emotionally insecure and your home was a broken one, your dreams may still reflect confusion and fear from that period. You may carry your psychic struggles over into your own marriage, creating problems that should not exist. If this is the case, give yourself a dream catharsis in which you examine your dreams and try to rationalize the experiences that led to them. Try to work out your problems with your mate or go to a marriage counselor to help you find solutions to sexual or other incompatibility problems that exist in your marriage.

7. Some of the dream symbols that signal romantic difficulties may be earthquakes or floods in which everything is threatened with ruin. You may find yourself in a terrifying situation where buildings are tumbling down or flood waters are swirling around you, threatening to carry your home away. You may be running to get away from an earthquake when the earth opens up and swallows you. (This may be a symbol of being buried alive in a marriage that is no longer fulfilling and satisfying.)

In such drastic instances, try to get out of the marriage if there are no children involved, and work out your marital problems with the air of a psychologist or psychiatrist. The trauma of a broken marriage is less harmful than the frustrating life of misery and incompletion that accompanies an unhappy marriage.

8. Begin a dream diary in which you write down the details of a perfect romance or marriage. Jot down your ideas just before going to bed, and then read this dream diary over every night, imprinting these thoughts onto the sensitive psychic mind so that it can guide you, through your dreams, to a happier love life.

Also keep track of your dreams in this diary; jot them down when you awaken so that you can read them over the next day and analyze their contents. In this way, if the same themes keep recurring in your dreams, you will know that your psychic twin is trying to give you some important message that could change your romantic or marital situation.

In this dream diary tell your psychic twin the type of person you want as a romantic partner. Give the mental characteristics, the education, the ethnic background, and then list the various experiences you would like to enjoy with this dream lover. Soon your dreams will begin to mirror these psychic images and your psychic twin will get busy pushing you in the direction where these dream fantasies can become reality.

REVIEW OF POINTS IN CHAPTER ELEVEN

1. Can you attain in reality the universal dream of finding the perfect soul mate and living happily ever after?
2. Scientific analysis shows that our dreams accurately reflect the events of our emotional lives, and in turn our lives shape our nightly dreams.
3. A fifteen-year-old girl had fantasies in which her handsome young brother-in-law made love to her. This dream became a reality one night when he visited her room.
4. You can shape the events of your romantic life in your dreams and project them to the outer world of reality by using your psychic twin to carry our your mental concepts.
5. You can give instructions to your psychic twin about the type of soul mate you want to find and then receive psychic guidance to find your perfect soul mate.
6. Dream symbols that indicate romantic fulfillment include dreaming of a church, an altar, a wedding gown or cake, or seeing oneself on a honeymoon with one's dream lover.
7. Seek out real-life situations that will carry out your desirable dream-fantasies. Go to the places where such people usually congregate, for like attracts like.
8. One young woman projected the dream fantasy of her soul mate by dreaming of flying to Hawaii. She flew there and on the third day met her dream lover.
9. You can give various suggestions to your psychic twin each night when you go to sleep, asking for guidance to meeting your soul mate.
10. Troubled dreams reflecting frustration and obstacles in

your path could relate to an unhappy and unsatisfactory sex life in or out of marriage.

11. A woman's sexual fantasies followed her into her dream world, where she saw herself at a "disrobing" party in which couples swapped lovers. She found herself enjoying this dream fantasy, which came true when she and her husband did go to such a party.

12. Young people mold their love lives and marriages after the examples set by their parents. If your early years were happy and your parents remained together in love, chances are that you will have a happy love life.

13. Children from broken homes have troubled nightmares of being pursued in winding tunnels or being lost in dark forests where strange creatures wait to pounce on them.

14. If you experienced emotional insecurity in your early life, you can use dream catharsis to clear your psychic slate of all such disturbing remembrances and reprogram yourself to new, happy, and loving relationships in your real life.

12
COMMAND AND CONTROL PEOPLE THROUGH DREAM HYPNOSIS

In recent experiments with hypnosis, scientists have come across some fascinating facts that were not previously known.

During the sleeping stages, a person possesses more ESP and psychic awareness than in his so-called natural waking state. He is able to send and receive telepathic messages with greater accuracy. The hypnotized person often has precognition—the ability to accurately know future events that are still hidden in the matrix of time. He can cross mysterious frontiers of time and space and project himself into geographical areas he has never visited in real life.

Dream hypnosis is an artificially induced state of sleep in which your conscious mind is suspended for a short time and your subconscious is then free to carry out instructions and commands that you have given it in your waking state.

To achieve dream hypnosis you must literally put yourself into a kind of trance, where you are programmed to carry out certain instructions that have been given to the higher, psychic mind.

Edgar Cayce Used Dream Hypnosis to Discover Illness

I had occasion to meet Edgar Cayce once when I was lecturing in Carnegie Hall, and I was impressed by his ability to put himself into a state of self-induced hypnosis, like a trance, where his other mind could penetrate the aura of people who were sick. In that state of trance Cayce could accurately diagnose a person's illness, and even doctors were baffled at his uncanny accuracy.

In my many years of investigation of psychic phenomena, I found out that everyone can use this power of dream hypnosis for many different purposes. Here are some of the things you can expect to do when you have mastered this technique.

1. You will be able to enter the dream world that has no dimensions of time and space and influence the minds of others to carry out certain actions.
2. You can use dream hypnosis to penetrate the aura of some person who has a bad habit, such as smoking, drug addiction, or alcoholism, and command that person to give up his destructive habit.
3. You will have the power to imprint your creative ideas on the minds of those in your office, home, or social circles and have these ideas carried out to your and their benefit.
4. You can bring other people into the aura of your romantic dream hypnosis and make them love you. (If the person is absolutely not compatible with you, your higher mind will instantly know this and neutralize the hypnotic magnetism.)
5. You can mentally project your thoughts into a person's mind and find out if he is dishonest, if he is cheating on you in marriage, or if he is stealing from you in business.
6. You can use dream hypnosis to enter into the mind of your employer and command him to give you a raise in salary or to advance you in your position. (Of course, if you are not worth more money, you cannot force him to give you a higher salary.)
7. You can use dream hypnosis to probe the secrets of the universe, to discover places where oil, gold, uranium, or other precious elements are hidden. You can use it to discover chemical formulas that might make you rich.
8. In dream hypnosis you can project yourself to places where money may be hidden or discover methods for winning at games of chance or drawing the winning lottery ticket.
9. In dream hypnosis you can influence wealthy friends to give you valuable gifts such as jewelry, furs, or cars.

10. You can use dream hypnosis if you are a salesperson and want to sell more insurance policies, merchandise, or other things of value.

11. You can also use dream hypnosis to help you solve your problems or show you how to write great novels, invent useful objects, compose beautiful music, or paint masterpieces.

Before you try to project your mind to command and control others through dream hypnosis, you must first learn how to put yourself into the sensitized and impressionable state of consciousness that will release your own psychic mind while you are in a suspended, dreamlike state known as a trance or self-hypnosis.

HOW TO USE DREAM HYPNOSIS DURING YOUR WAKING HOURS

You can use dream hypnosis during the day while you are wide-awake, or you can use it at night while you are sleeping, letting your soul reach out into "the invisible, some letter of that after-life to spell," as Omar Khayyam said. If you are in the waking state you can go into a self-induced state of hypnosis in which your higher psychic mind will become the automatic guiding light that reaches out and touches the minds of others.

You do not need to worry about whether your thoughts are really penetrating the minds or auras of other people. You can be sure that when these people are in a moment of reverie, or when they are asleep and their conscious guards are down, your thoughts will penetrate their consciousness and make them aware of your hypnotic commands.

To put yourself into a state of dream hypnosis, sit quietly where you will not be disturbed for at least half an hour. Then relax your body completely by simply saying "peace, peace, peace," over and over. Or you can say "relax, relax, relax." Keep your eyes open for a few moments, looking at a bright object fixed about two or three feet above your head. Or you can look at a spot on the wall that is above eye level.

When you have intoned the mantra *peace* about ten times and you really feel relaxed, close your eyes and prepare yourself for going into a self-induced trance, a process that scientists call self-hypnosis. After a little practice you can go into a state of self-hypnosis almost instantly by saying some key word like *peace* or *relax*.

Repeat the following words or thoughts softly under your breath until you feel lulled into a state of complete peace and relaxation, almost as if you are going to sleep:

Peace—peace—peace. I now relax my mind and body and I am in a state of perfect peace and poise and power. I command my subconscious to take over the functions of consciousness. I now wish to project my psychic mind power to the minds of others so that they will carry out my commands and fulfill my wishes. I desire only that which is for my own good and the good of others. I will use my higher psychic power only for moral, lawful, and constructive acts, and I will not ask anything of others that I would not do myself.

Now when you begin to feel drowsy, keep your eyes closed, and you are ready through mental telepathy to project the mind and soul power that will reach out and command and control the minds of others. We shall now study each command in turn. These can be expanded to include your personal preferences, and you may use different thoughts and words.

INFLUENCE OTHERS TO CARRY OUT YOUR DIRECTIONS

Choose the person you wish to command and control and call that person by name. This can be a mental projection in which you merely think the name and the commands, or it can be an oral one in which you make your commands in a strong but quiet voice. Let's use for an example a wife trying to reach into the psyche of an inconsiderate and undemonstrative husband.

John, I am now sending you thoughts that I want lodged in your psychic mind centers while you sleep tonight. I want you to act on these commands, as I know they are for your own good. I want you to be a more loving person, to show more affection in our marriage, to not let your mother influence you against me. I direct you to respond to my love with more affection, to tell me you love me more often, to show more attention to the children. I want you to be more ambitious and try to get advances in your work so that we can have the better things in life. You know I love you more than anyone else in the world, and I want you to love me in the same way.

Now, after you have programmed the above statements, or others that fit your own personal needs, into your psychic mind, you can come out of your self-hypnotic state, go about your regular activities, and forget what you have done. If you are doing this at night, just before going to sleep, do not go on too long but make your powerful statements to yourself. Even if your mate is lying alongside of you, it can be done in silence and he or she need never know. Then drift off to sleep, confident that your soul and the soul of the person you are projecting to will in some mysterious manner meet and exchange ideas on the astral planes, for "soul speaks to soul, as star to star."

COMMAND A PERSON WHO HAS A BAD HABIT TO GIVE IT UP

——(Call the person by name), I am projecting my thoughts to you, asking that your higher psychic mind will know that I am concerned for your health and welfare and want only the best for you. You know that your habit (here mention the habit: smoking, alcoholism, drug addiction, gambling, laziness, procrastination, selfishness, inconsideration) is harming you. You will have a deep desire to give up this bad habit, to live a more healthy, happy, and prosperous life. In a short time you will tell me that you no longer crave this habit and that you are giving it up for good.

Generally, this type of dream hypnosis has an effect on the person with a bad habit because the person's higher psychic mind is already aware of the fact that it is causing him problems and should be given up.

A Mother Used Dream Hypnosis to Stop Her Son's Smoking

A woman had a sixteen-year-old son who had taken up cigarette smoking. She decided to use our dream hypnosis technique to make the boy give up smoking voluntarily.

She projected these hypnotic thoughts each night, visualizing her son's face as she drifted off to sleep. Then in her dreams she had visions that her son was going to stop smoking and would tell her of his decision in a few days.

Sure enough, within one week, when the boy was sitting at the breakfast table and had finished eating, he lit up a cigarette, puffed on it a few times, and then said, "I don't know why, but this cigarette tastes bitter to me. I'm going to stop smoking."

You can reach the minds of those who are emotionally close to you, such as your children, your mate, and your relatives, much better than strangers. But to use dream hypnosis successfully, you must practice it over and over until you have achieved proficiency in the art of putting yourself into a trance and letting your higher psychic mind take over, projecting your thoughts under the laws that rule extrasensory perception.

IMPRINT YOUR CREATIVE IDEAS ON THE MINDS OF OTHERS FOR YOUR AND THEIR BENEFIT

Use this dream projection for your fellow workers to imprint them with ideas of harmony, cooperation, and love:

I now project to my coworkers the following thoughts: You will all work in harmony and peace with me. We shall share in a cooperative effort to make our business a success and to increase sales and promote expansion. As our business prospers, so too we shall prosper.

Use this projection for your family relationships:

I project my thoughts to my home environment, asking that all the members of my family live in peace and harmony and love with each other. We shall have mutual respect for each other and give as well as take, expressing our appreciation for those things we sometimes take for granted.

Use this projection for your friends:

I wish to project my thoughts towards having a successful social life. I now imprint on the minds of my friends in my social circle the knowledge that I admire them, respect them, and wish to continue in our present relationship, overcoming all animosity, scandal, or discord that might arise in our future relationships.

BRING OTHERS INTO THE AURA OF YOUR ROMANTIC DREAM AND MAKE THEM LOVE YOU

You can use this dream projection in a general way, to make everyone admire and love you, or you can specifically project it to some individual that you want to magnetize towards loving you.

I now project my loving thoughts to you, with the intent of influencing you to love me and desire me as I love and desire you. I have only thoughts of good for you, and I desire the best in life for you and me. If you feel that I am your true soul mate, respond with signs that I will understand. I wish to marry you and have a home where we can rear our family in comfort and security. I will always act in an honorable and honest manner and work for your future interests, as I know you will work for mine. Tell me that you love me and that you want me as your romantic partner for the future.

This Woman Attracted Her Soul Mate through Dream Hypnosis

There was a member of our lecture group in Los Angeles who studied these techniques of using dream hypnosis and who, having had two marriages that failed, wanted to attract her true soul mate.

She programmed her psychic mind with dream hypnosis and each night when she went to bed she projected her romantic desires to a man she had recently met when she bought a home in the Hollywood Hills. He worked in a real estate office and had shown her her home; he was courteous and attentive, and she felt that he was romantically attracted to her. Her female intuition told her she could really love him, yet she did not know how to make him love her.

She worked on her dream hypnosis for one week before there was any response. One day a car pulled up in the driveway. It was the real estate salesman! He said, "I had an urge to come up and see you today. I want to know if everything about the house is satisfactory and if there is anything further I can do for you."

Of course, this was the very thing this woman had been projecting: that he would seek her out. Before he was finished that day he asked her to have lunch with him at the Polo Lounge of the Beverly Hills Hotel, and that was the beginning of the fulfillment of her romantic dream. This man fell in love with her, she later told me, almost like a person who was hypnotized, using the very words and phrases when he proposed marriage that she had projected to him, and even suggesting that they go to Hawaii on their honeymoon—the very place she had projected in her dream hypnosis!

FIND OUT IF A PERSON IS CHEATING ON YOU

You can project your dream-self into a person's aura and have psychic empathy with him by putting yourself into a trance and commanding your higher psychic mind to project you on a secret mission into his aura to discover if he is treacherous and dishonest.

Tell your higher psychic mind, just before going to sleep each night, something like the following:

I wish to have secret information about ———. Is this person being honest with me or lying? Is he trying to conceal things from me? Can I trust him in my business? Reveal his true character, and if he is cheating me or lying to me, let him expose himself in such a way that I shall know beyond the shadow of a doubt.

A woman in our classes in New York City had reason to believe that her husband was cheating on her and having an affair with another woman. She had never been able to catch him, so she tried using dream hypnosis to have him give himself away if he were really being untrue to her.

She projected the mental picture that he would become confused in some way and reveal his secret romance. This went on for a few days, and one night she had the impulse to go through his coat pocket while he slept. There she found a romantic note a girl had written to her husband, telling him how she loved him and wanted to marry him. The girl worked in her husband's office. She had carelessly written him a note, and under the influence of the wife's dream hypnosis, the husband had absentmindedly left the note in his pocket!

USE DREAM HYPNOSIS TO COMMAND YOUR EMPLOYER TO PROMOTE YOU

If you feel that you are worth more money or that you should be promoted in your job and your employer has not yielded to your reasonable demands, try using dream hypnosis to ask for a raise or to seek advancement to a better position.

When in your trancelike state, project thoughts like these, using your boss's name.

———, *you know that I am worth more money than you are paying me. I now ask for $10 a week raise in salary to meet rising costs of living. I also wish to be made manager of this department. You know that I have the ability to be extremely valuable to the firm. You will voluntarily seek me out and advise me that, starting immediately, I shall get my raise.*

One secretary practiced her dream hypnosis three times a day for one week before she had results: when she got up in the morning, during her lunch hours, and just before going to bed at night. She went into her boss's office to take dictation one day, and he was sitting at his desk looking as if he were hypnotized, she later told me. Then he said in a flat monotone, "I don't know why I'm doing this damned fool thing, but I'm giving you a $10 a week raise in salary."

Two months later, she was advanced to an executive position at an even higher salary!

FIND OIL, GOLD, URANIUM, COAL, OR OTHER PRECIOUS MATERIALS

You can use dream hypnosis in a general way to contact the cosmic mind that can reveal the hidden places where treasures exist. I know an instance from life of a prospector in the Nevada desert in the early 1930s who used this dream hypnosis technique by constantly asking his higher mind to guide him to a gold mine. He had this secret dream for several years before he was finally led to a section of Nevada near Las Vegas, which was then only a small town, and there he found a gold mine that brought him five million dollars in the next five years! This was the famous Johnny Mine, owned by O. T. Johnson, one of the early pioneer families of Los Angeles that founded their real estate holdings from the money they made in mining.

Here are some statements to make for programming your higher psychic mind with this desire for finding hidden treasures.

I now command the higher psychic forces within my mind to guide me to finding hidden treasures in the earth. I know that the earth is filled with deposits of iron, coal, silver, gold, uranium, and platinum, and I wish to discover my own source of infinite wealth, so that I may use my money to do good for the world.

WIN AT THE RACES, GAMBLING, AND LOTTERIES AND FIND HIDDEN MONEY

Very often your higher psychic mind knows winning techniques for games of chance like roulette, twenty-one, poker, dice, or the lottery that could make a big stake for your future fortune.

Recently a New Jersey man won the million-dollar lottery by dreaming of the winning numbers. He bought the ticket with those numbers and admitted in a newspaper interview that he had a dream in which he saw those numbers!

Most gamblers use this dream hypnosis subconsciously without being aware of it. The dice thrower warms the dice, talks to them affectionately, and commands them to come up seven or eleven. I have seen this happen in four consecutive rolls for a person who was "hot" and having a winning run.

Sometimes this higher psychic mind knows the winning horse in a race, for the computer of the higher mind assimilates all the information about a horse and then projects to the conscious the name of the winner. I have known people at the races who won consistently because they had programmed themselves to win.

Dream Hypnosis Won This Woman $10,000

A woman had been projecting a desire for $10,000 for some time to pay her debts and get rid of a mortgage on her small home. One day at an auction she bought an upholstered chair that no one else seemed to want. After she had had it in her living room a few days she decided to change the upholstery to match the rest of her furniture. She removed the old faded upholstery, and there beneath the material she found the sum of $10,000 in big bills—the exact amount she had demanded from her higher psychic forces.

Use this type of statement to program yourself for winning money or finding hidden wealth:

I now command my psychic mind to guide me to hidden sources of money. I wish to find some winning system so that I can make a lot of money fast. I would like to have the sum of $50,000 to give me financial security for the future. Reveal for me a winning number at the lottery or a winning system at roulette, dice, cards, or horse racing that can make me financially independent.

INFLUENCE WEALTHY FRIENDS TO GIVE YOU VALUABLE GIFTS

Everyone knows people who are more wealthy than they are. You may not know millionaires like Rockefeller or J. Paul Getty, but somewhere in your future you will come across people who might be influenced through dream hypnosis to give you valuable gifts.

A woman recently projected her desire for a beautiful Cadillac. She was magnetized to Elvis Presley, to whom she told her impossible dream, and the generous singer made her a gift of the car!

A man I knew, who had studied this technique in my classes, projected the dream that he wanted an RCA color TV set. He could not afford to pay the large sum it cost, so he worked on his dream hypnosis with the cosmic mind, projecting the thought that somehow, someone would make it possible for him to have the TV set. In two weeks some neighbors in the same apartment house, who were moving to California, sold him their nearly new RCA color TV set for only $100.

Here are the statements you can project for influencing wealthy persons to give you money or gifts of value.

I project the desire for jewels, tape recorders, a TV set, and other things of value that I wish to have as gifts from those who can afford it. I shall be willing to give something of value in return, and I now ask that these persons be magnetized into my aura for our mutual good.

BECOME A SUPERSALESPERSON

I want to become a supersalesperson and I now wish to command and control those I meet to listen to my sales talk and to respond in a positive manner, buying my products without resistance.

I now ask that my higher psychic mind give me the right persuasive words to use in presenting my sales talk to the prospective buyer. I shall use the hypnotic eye and look at the person without blinking. My voice shall convey the impression of honesty and integrity, inspiring my customer with confidence in me and my product. I wish to make ten sales today and increase my income so that I can make the sum of $50,000 or more a year.

SOLVE PROBLEMS, WRITE NOVELS, COMPOSE MUSIC, INVENT OBJECTS, OR PAINT MASTERPIECES

This higher psychic mind that you can program through dream hypnosis knows how to put together astounding inventions, or discover formulas that can make you rich. It has all the pieces of the mysterious puzzle of life within its hidden memory paths and genetic patterns of consciousness. To release this mystical creative power, use the following programming statement:

I now tap the creative power of my higher psychic centers. I ask for the release of a superpower to create a great destiny. I wish to be shown how to find my own hidden potentials of genius and how to use them to build a great destiny in the creative arts. I wish to use this power to solve my daily problems; to be guided to new business ventures that bring me profit; and to discover methods for utilizing my potentials to bring me fame and fortune.

When you have spent several months in programming your psychic mind centers with these dream hypnosis techniques, you will become so sensitized to your environment and to the people around you that you will instantly sense a situation that could benefit you. You will be given strange and unusual dreams that are symbols of your new state of higher awareness. You will have achieved what mystics call "cosmic consciousness," which all geniuses of history had when they made their great discoveries and were guided to the achievement of deeds that changed the course of history.

REVIEW OF POINTS IN CHAPTER TWELVE

1. Psychic powers and ESP awareness are greatly increased when a person is under hypnosis or in a state of self-induced trance or self-hypnosis.
2. Edgar Cayce, the "sleeping prophet," could go into a self-induced trance or dream hypnosis and accurately diagnose a patient's ailments.
3. Through dream hypnosis, one can enter the dream world that has no dimensions of time and space and produce miracles.
4. You can enter the state of dream hypnosis and use mantras through meditation to achieve control of your higher psychic mind.
5. You can use dream hypnosis to influence the minds of others and command them to carry out your instructions perfectly.
6. Dream hypnotic statements can help a person overcome bad habits like smoking, drinking, or drug addiction and change his habit patterns voluntarily.
7. A mother used dream hypnosis to influence her sixteen-year-old son to break his harmful smoking habit within one week.
8. You can use dream hypnosis to imprint your creative ideas

on the minds of others and cause them to take action that proves beneficial for you and themselves.

9. You can use dream hypnosis to enter the auras of others, and imprint romantic ideas that make them love you and want to marry you.

10. A woman in California used dream hypnosis to attract her perfect soul mate. When he proposed to her, he even used the words she had projected, and he suggested for their honeymoon the very place she had mentally selected!

11. You can use dream hypnosis to find out if your mate is cheating on you or if a person in business is dishonest with you.

12. A woman used dream hypnosis to discover that her husband was having an affair with a girl in his office.

13. You can command your employer to give you a raise in salary or to promote you to an executive job by projecting the ideas to him through dream hypnosis.

14. Dream hypnosis can be used to find gold, coal, oil, uranium, or other precious materials in nature.

15. A man was guided to finding a five-million-dollar gold mine by programming his psychic centers through dream hypnosis.

16. You can win at games of chance, horse races, cards, dice, roulette, and lotteries. A man won the million-dollar lottery in New Jersey recently after he dreamed the winning numbers.

17. A woman projected to her dream-self that she needed the sum of $10,000. She was guided in the most mysterious manner to finding this amount of cash.

18. You can use dream hypnosis to influence wealthy persons to help you, to become a supersalesperson, to solve problems, and to achieve fulfillment of your potential for creativity.

13
MIRACLE HEALING THROUGH DREAM THERAPY

Just as psychologists and psychiatrists use a patient's dreams to probe the sources of mental illness, so too a doctor versed in psychic dreamology can use a patient's dreams to find out what is wrong with him and then prescribe a treatment that is based on knowledge of the subconscious.

In a fairly new science known as zone therapy, various organs of the body are supposed to have their functioning power in certain areas of the brain. When these areas are congested or the nerves are short-circuited, illness develops in the various organs controlled by these brain areas.

ACUPUNCTURE AND ZONE THERAPY

In recent years the miraculous results achieved by acupuncture seem to prove that there is something to zone therapy and that dreams could stimulate these hidden areas of the body, resulting in the releasing of healing power in various organs of the body.

Wonderful results have been achieved in healing through meditation sessions where the patient closes his eyes and goes into a trancelike state for fifteen minutes, three times a day. This seems to indicate that something remarkable occurs when the conscious mind is stilled and the subconscious mind is allowed to take over and do the work of healing.

Even the miracles of Jesus were ascribed by the Master Himself, not to His own power, but to "the Father within, who doeth the work." This could relate only to a superior mental and spiritual power that is above and beyond the limited conscious mind.

In order to utilize this subconscious power for healing and for keeping your body healthy so that you can live to a natural and healthy old age, it is essential that you understand the miraculous powers of your subconscious.

Your Mother's Subconscious Built Your Body in Nine Months

Before you were born your mother's subconscious was busy building your body in her womb. Think of the miracle that took place in that short period of nine months! Her subconscious knew all the secrets of chemistry that could utilize the materials it needed from her bloodstream, to fashion the lungs, the nervous system, heart, kidneys, stomach, and eyes, ears, and brain. Then it surrounded the entire embryonic child with a skin that had millions of pores arranged so that it could breathe through the skin when it was born. It sealed this miraculous little creature in a watery element, like a fish that had gills and that did not look at all like a human being in those first few weeks. In fact, scientists tell us that an embryologist examining the first-formed fetus of a horse, a snake, or a human being would be hard put to tell which was which! Only after a few weeks of growth does this amazing intelligence of the subconscious imprint upon the fetus the identity of a human being.

Can you not trust this mysterious higher mind that built your body with the care and healing of your physical and mental self? You can motivate this higher mind at will and use psychic dreamology to heal you if you should be sick and to keep your body healthy, vital, youthful and strong.

Before you begin to use dream therapy for healing, you should realize that most faith healing occurs when a person is in a state of self-hypnosis; he believes that he is going to be healed by prayer, or by a lucky talisman, or through the ministrations of a person reputed to have miraculous powers. In this state of highly charged emotional intensity, the conscious mind is somehow bypassed, and the subconscious or superconscious is brought into action, performing the actual healing of the sick person.

A Woman Healed of Tuberculosis through Dream Therapy

Dr. Alexis Carrel told of a young woman who was very sick with tuberculosis of the abdomen and was beyond medical help. She rallied out of a coma one day and asked that she brought to the miracle grotto at Lourdes, where many sick people have been healed.

When she was placed on a stretcher at the edge of the grotto, she went into a deep, trancelike sleep, losing all consciousness. Waters from the grotto were used to bathe her abdomen, and the doctors who had carefully examined her before this experience patiently waited to see what results would occur.

Within a short time the young woman opened her eyes and remarked, "I am healed, and I shall devote my life to helping humanity by joining a church order and becoming a nun." She rose from the stretcher and walked, something she had not done for many days. The doctors, including Alexis Carrel, examined her carefully and found no trace of the deadly tuberculosis that had seemed fatal!

ALPHA BIOFEEDBACK AND MEDITATION

In recent experiments with alpha biofeedback and meditation, in which a person puts himself into a kind of trance by reciting certain mantras or prayers, it has been observed that the blood pressure changes, the metabolism is affected, the heartbeat can be regulated to beat slow or fast, the skin resistance is lowered to electrical charges, and other mental and physiological changes occur that show something vitally dramatic is happening to the mind and body.

Psychic Trance among the Holy Men of India

In my own trips to India and other countries of the Far East and Middle East, I have personally seen holy men walk barefooted over red-hot coals without being injured. I have seen them after being buried alive for several days without air, water, or food come out thinner but perfectly healthy. I noted that before undergoing these rigorous tests these holy men went into a trancelike state by reciting mantras, chanting certain phrases, and controlling their breathing to make it slower.

Mahatma Gandhi and Psychic Somnambulism

On one of my earlier trips to India I met Mahatma Gandhi and discovered that in what he called psychic somnambulism he could hypnotize himself and put himself into a state where his conscious mind was out of the way, letting his subconscious take over. In these states of meditation Gandhi could go without food for many days without suffering any ill effects.

When Gandhi was assassinated at the age of seventy-seven, the doctors who viewed his body at the autopsy said he was in perfect condition and that his body was like that of a man of thirty.

PSYCHIC DREAMS THAT WARN OF ILLNESS

Dreams of various forms of illness often precede the actual sickness itself. The congested organ often communicates its message to your subconscious for help. Then the psychic centers release this request to your dream-self, using symbols that can be interpreted by those versed in the science of dreamology.

Some common forms of dreams that could be warning of impending illness are the following:

You may dream that you are being operated on for some nameless disease with the accompanying fear that the doctors may perform the wrong kind of operation or remove some organ other than the diseased one. This often indicates that there is some condition in the body that it will be necessary to remove by surgery. The section of the body that the dreams relate to is the place to look for the disturbance.

A dream in which the heart has stopped beating, bringing about a feeling of suffocation, and that the breath has stopped often causes one to wake up in alarm. The heart then begins to pound and the breathing is accelerated, as though the subconscious is warning that some heart condition may be threatening the person.

A Dream Warned Her of Approaching Cataracts

A woman who was in our lecture group once told me that she kept having a dream in which she wore a mask over her face and that it was difficult for her to see where she was going. She found herself stumbling and falling frequently. Soon after, in real life, when her eyes began to give her trouble she went to her doctor and found that she was developing cataracts on both eyes. Later, she was operated on and given treatment that saved her from blindness.

His Dreams Revealed a Brain Tumor

One man had a feeling that his head was filled with bees while he slept and dreamed. This dream sometimes caused him to awaken with buzzing sensations in his head; sometimes his head felt hot and in his dreams it would explode, awakening him with a feeling of impending catastrophe. A few weeks later this man developed strange symptoms of dizziness, and he would lose his balance and nearly fall over. Sometimes he would pass out and awaken later, not knowing what happened to him.

An examination and X-rays proved that he had a small tumor in his brain that required removal by surgery. Had he known something about the interpretation of dreams, he might have been able to avoid waiting so long before seeking medical help.

Dreams about death in various forms can signify that the person is actually developing a condition in his body that might produce serious illness or even death. A woman who kept dreaming that she was dying of cancer was later examined and found to have cancer. An operation and radiation therapy saved her life.

Her Dreams Warned Her of Glandular Imbalance

Sometimes the dream will be that of a person being paralyzed, unable to move or call for help. This could indicate something physically wrong that requires attention.

One woman had a recurring dream in which she would begin to swell up like a balloon and she feared that she would float away from earth. Her subconscious was trying to warn her of a metabolic and glandular condition that required help. Later, she did swell up from the wrong diet and accumulations of water, and the doctors had to work with gland therapy and other forms of treatment to remove the physical cause of her ailment.

We can learn how to program the subconscious so that it works at night with dream therapy to heal the body should we become sick. We can also condition the subconscious to keep us healthy. It has now been found that hypnosis helps treat many different forms of illness, especially those due to psychosomatic causes arising from emotional upsets such as anger, hatred, hostility, and fear. Experiments performed with rats in laboratories prove that almost every type of ailment that afflicts human beings can also be given to rats when they are agitated and put under conditions of stress, such as fear, worry, noise, confusion. These rats develop high blood pressure, heart trouble, cancer, arthritis, and many mental conditions, just as human beings do.

Obviously, to remove these emotional causes of disease is to assure a person that he will be healthy and avoid the complications that often come about because of emotional stress.

REGIMEN FOR USING DREAM THERAPY FOR HEALING

1. Just before you go to sleep each night, program your subconscious with suggestions of health, youth, vitality, and long life. Tell your psychic twin to work while you sleep to regulate your metabolism, to control the secretions of your glands, to

digest your food and assimilate it perfectly, to remove the fatigue acids from your bloodstream, to replace the worn-out cells with new ones, and to insulate your body against the invasion of harmful germs.

Your programming statement can be as follows, or you can make up one of your own to fit your exact needs.

I now program my subconscious to work while I sleep, to heal my body of any and all negative conditions. I ask that it remove unwanted chemicals and insulate my body against the invasion of germs. My glands shall secrete their chemicals perfectly, giving my body all the elements it needs to sustain it in perfect health.

I ask my subconscious to regulate my blood pressure, causing it to be normal for my age and condition. I ask that my heartbeat be regulated to approximately seventy-two beats a minute and that it send nourishment to all organs of my body, causing them to function perfectly.

I am healthy. I am strong and vital. I am young. I wish to live to be 100 years and to have perfect health. If any conditions of arthritis or other ailments exist, I ask my subconscious to remove these negative forces and restore me to perfect health.

2. After you have given your subconscious the above type of instructions to carry out while you sleep, you can direct the life energy and healing power to various parts of the body and its vital organs.

After you have given your subconscious these suggestions, you can keep your eyes closed while you visualize your heart. Make a fist, and know that this is about the size of your heart. Then open and close your fist approximately seventy-two times a minute, and talk to your heart, softly and slowly, like this:

You will now beat at a normal rate, pumping the lifeblood and nourishment to every cell of my brain and body. You will remove all poisons from my bloodstream through the kidneys, and you will pump the life force through my body perfectly. As you beat, you will become stronger and resist the erosion of my negative emotions. While I sleep you will be the guardian angel of my life, keeping me in perfect health.

3. Condition your psychic twin to give you revealing dreams of anything that might be wrong with your body. Caution it to warn

you of weaknesses in any body organ; urge it to reveal, through symbols and direct messages, any hidden glandular or other condition that might require attention. Tell your psychic twin to be on the lookout and to warn you in dreams of malfunctioning of any organ, or metabolic defects; to give you guidance as to the elements the body needs for repairing its cells and giving you good health; and to remove all excessive calcium or other negative elements that might give you various diseases like arthritis or rheumatism. Specifically urge the subconscious to dissolve any and all attempts of cancerous cells to gain control of your body, giving you warning if they should be present.

4. There is a self-immunizing process that goes on constantly in your body that should keep you healthy. This immunization occurs only when there are no forces such as emotional stress or chemical poisoning that interfere with its normal functioning. Some scientists now believe that everyone has cancer cells working in his body at some time or another. The person who finally winds up having the disease is the one in whom the immunizing mechanism has failed so that the cells multiply and grow. Those who are using this immunizing factor are the people who live in a relaxed state, whose diet is balanced and nutritious, and who use mental therapy to arrest the inroads of this disease or any other form of illness.

To strengthen this self-immunizing power of your subconscious, use the following self-hypnotic statements to reach into your psyche, causing it to release the right chemicals that will immunize you:

I now ask my subconscious to release the elements my body needs to immunize me against all forms of sickness. I shall be relaxed and avoid all conditions of haste, stress, and emotional strain, giving my body the necessary climate for this immunizing process to work perfectly.

5. Just before you drift off to sleep, after giving yourself this form of self-hypnosis and dream therapy, tell your psychic twin to take you into the realm of dreams where it can talk to you through beautiful symbols and mental images and give you interesting dream experiences, pleasant emotions, and restful situations. After a night of such healing and beautiful dreams,

you will awake rested and refreshed, able to take on your day's normal problems and challenges.

In this way you will mentally clean the slate each night, and your dreams will begin to act as a catharsis, driving out the nightmare images of fear, anxiety, insanity, fear of death, accident, tragedy, war, prison, being buried alive, and other dreams that are symptomatic of bodily distress and illness.

REVIEW OF POINTS IN CHAPTER THIRTEEN

1. Through psychic dreamology a doctor can probe a patient's dreams and discover hidden weaknesses and sickness in a person's body and then prescribe treatment for the condition.
2. Zone therapy and acupuncture seem to prove that various areas of the body respond to mental impulses, which control the nerves and body organs.
3. The subconscious knows all the secrets of body chemistry and can release healing power in any part of the body when it is programmed through dream therapy.
4. In faith healing the patient goes into a dreamlike, otherworldly state of consciousness, removing the tensions and stresses and allowing his subconscious to do the actual work of healing.
5. At the shrine of Lourdes a woman who had tuberculosis of the stomach was completely healed while in a trance. She believed that the healing waters would work a miracle.
6. The recent scientific approach to alpha biofeedback, brainwave therapy, meditation, and other techniques use this form of dream therapy to achieve their healing miracles.
7. Holy men in India can walk over red-hot coals barefooted and not be injured because they have put themselves into a self-induced state of trance in which the body is immunized against pain.
8. A woman who dreamed frequently of having a mask over her face and not being able to see later developed cataracts that required surgery in both eyes.
9. Various types of dreams indicate that there is something

wrong with the physical body. They can be messages from your psychic twin to indicate that your body requires treatment.

10. You can program your subconscious with dream therapy so that your body will be given healing treatments while you sleep.

11. Self-hypnosis has been found to heal many forms of illness. Stress conditions often bring on heart trouble, high blood pressure, and other ailments.

12. You can give programming statements to your psychic twin each night before you go to sleep so that it can work through your dreams to keep you healthy or heal you if you are sick.

13. You can build the self-immunizing processes of your body so that you can be saved from various diseases by programming this process into your dreams at night.

14

ASTRAL PROJECTION: THE ULTIMATE DREAM OF YOUR SOUL'S REMEMBRANCES

There is a mystical boundary that man reaches in his journey through life, which must ultimately include the soul and its remembrances. We go beyond that invisible borderline between spirit and matter the moment we enter into the dream world. There are mysterious occurrences in that dimension of time and space to which the mystics refer as the astral plane, where the soul has its own experiences while we sleep.

These ancients of the Far East, India, Tibet, China, Egypt, and Greece believed that there was a divine essence within man's soul that enabled him to explore these astral planes and discover the secrets of the universe. They taught that man's soul can travel backwards or forwards in time and not only review past events but accurately divine future events. On these astral planes the soul becomes attuned to the soul of the universe and has cosmic awareness. All knowledge is then apprehended; all power can be invoked. As the soul is a reflector of the divine intelligence, these mystics believed it could be transported instantaneously to any dimension of past or future time and space and read what they called the "akashic record," a kind of timetable listing the soul's experiences in other lives and its remembrances even before the human experience began.

FAMOUS HISTORICAL DREAMS

When we explore some of the revelations made during these astral journeys in so-called dreams of historical figures, we can hardly doubt that they were able to tap some astral realm where their souls received visions that changed the course of history. Let us study some of these, and then learn how we too may use astral projection, the ultimate dream of the soul's remembrances, to shape the tapestry of dreams that becomes our earthly destiny.

Joan of Arc, one of the most famous figures of history, had astral projections while she slept but also when awake. She heard voices and saw visions; she was told that she would lead the armies of France to victory against the enemy. Her prophetic dreams came true but misguided individuals, who thought her visions were from diabolical sources, had her burned to death.

A king's prophetic dream could be called an astral vision. King Philip of Macedon had a disturbing dream one night; in it he saw his wife's womb sealed off with a seal that bore the imprint of a lion, the symbol of royalty. He called in his wise men to interpret this strange dream, and they told him that his wife Olympia was pregnant and the dream was trying to reveal to the king that she would bear him a son. This astral vision came true with astounding accuracy, for Olympia did bear King Philip a son who became the legendary world conqueror Alexander the Great.

Many great events of history were revealed by astral dreams and visions. Even Alexander himself once had such a vision in which he saw that he would attack the city of Tyre and win. The event occurred exactly as his dream prophesied.

The great Persian leader King Cyrus had an astral vision in which he saw himself catching two suns. He consulted his wise men to see what the dream meant. They told him that he would rule Persia for two decades. Cyrus saw that prophecy come true, for he ruled over the Persian Empire for exactly two decades.

One of Julius Caesar's aides dreamed that the great leader would be attacked and advised him to "beware the Ides of March!" Caesar ignored the prophetic warning and went on with his plans; he was killed on the Ides of March.

MODERN INSTANCES OF DREAM PROPHECY

Such astral visions are not confined to the annals of history; right in our own century we have seen that "Your young men shall dream dreams, and your old men shall have visions," as the Bible tells us of the gift of astral projection, or the soul's prophetic warnings.

John F. Kennedy had a similar prophetic dream of his own assassination, and told this to members of his family before going to Dallas. One wonders why he did not take steps to avert this tragedy. We can rely on an answer that mystics would give us to that question. "It was Kennedy's karma," they would tell us, and his soul revealed the tragedy in advance to give him the power of choice, to avert the tragedy or to go along and pay the karmic debts that had piled up over the centuries. Certainly the tragedies that wiped out three Kennedy brothers seem to give some credence to the fact that a karmic curse has run its course, like a dark somber thread, through the tapestry of the Kennedys' lives. Even Ted Kennedy ultimately was not spared this karmic curse when he had his private tragedy where a young woman in his company lost her life by drowning.

REGIMEN TO USE ASTRAL PROJECTION

1. You can set the cosmic time clock of your future destiny by prerecording on your soul's akashic record events of your future, just as you can unwind the scrolls of past dimensions of time and view the soul's experiences. Even if you do not believe in reincarnation, on which the principles of astral projection are based, you can know the secrets of the universe, which have been stamped upon your immortal soul by a Divine Providence that has given to man some of his own divinity.

To develop the ability to project your soul on astral journeys while you sleep, prepare yourself when you go to bed for this mystical experience.

2. Instruct your higher self, the soul, to go out while you sleep and gather information, unravel mysteries, receive instruction and creative ideas, which it will reveal to you in the form of

vivid dreams. It is said that many masters in Tibet have the ability of actually transporting their astral selves to various places where they have been seen by many people as shadowy replicas of their earthly selves. This spiritual ectoplasm has been photographed by scientists in Russia and America. When a person makes his transition in what is called death, they have photographed the astral body rising above the physical body in the same shape and outline of the earthly, denser self. This divine essence in which the soul clothes itself can travel back into historical periods of time or project itself into the future and know events that are going to occur. Knowing the future is the art of precognition.

3. Breathe deeply ten or fifteen times before going into astral projection while you sleep. As the mind seems to operate under the same laws that govern electricity and magnetism, it was believed by the mystics of the past that breathing increased the fund of magnetic and electrical substance in the body and brain, making it easier for the soul to project into the astral realms.

4. Talk to this higher consciousness, your soul or spirit, as follows, using your own words or memorizing these, which will prepare your soul for its astral journey:

I now command my soul to go out into the astral realms while I sleep. I wish to discover secrets of my soul's mystical journey through time and space. If I have lived before, I wish to have revealed events of my past lives; the countries I have lived in; the experiences of history in which I have participated. I want information about the purpose of my life; why I have been born to suffer; what karmic lessons I am to learn in this earthly journey. I wish to become one with the mystery that has caught me up and have revealed for me the complete akashic record of my past and my future.

5. When you have given your soul these instructions, try to keep your eyes closed as you attempt the process known in astral projection as Exteriorization, releasing the soul from the gravity pull of your physical body and the earth. Then instruct your soul:

I wish to remember my astral dreams. When my journey is complete, I shall awaken with the return of my soul to my physical body.

6. Now you may feel a sense of lightness in your head, and the lower part of your body may seem to cease to exist, while you float as if on a cloud, with a feeling of rising up—up—up, like an airplane about to take off. When you are really exteriorizing, you may hear the sounds of celestial music that is not of this earth; you may see flashing bright colors that are beyond any you have known on earth; and you may see limitless space, as your soul rushes, like a spaceship, out into the infinite realms of time and space.

7. When you are really in orbit and out on the astral planes, you will experience a feeling of transcendental joy amounting to ecstasy. Your soul will have a sense of knowing all things and being in all places simultaneously. You will then begin to receive your transmission of the akashic record. It may be like a playback on videotape, in full color, showing the places you have formerly lived in. You may find yourself standing on the Egyptian plains, in the moonlight, before pyramids that tower above the sun-parched desert. You may find yourself a king or queen sitting on a throne, or a serf working in the fields; you may experience an entire lifetime in India, or see yourself building the Great Wall of China. These kaleidoscopic scenes will pass before your soul's vision, in the twinkling of an eye, just as they say a drowning man's lifetime passes in review.

Mystical Experiences of the Great Pyramid

Two years ago I had the pleasure of taking 100 of my lecture members from Los Angeles and New York City on a mystic quest to the Mideast, where we visited Egypt and Greece. Several members had been impelled to go on this quest, because they had astral visions of having lived in the days of the pharaohs in that land of mystery. They told me that after going up into the king's chamber of the giant pyramid, they had psychic messages confirming that they had indeed been a part of that vast pageant of history in the early days of Egyptian glory and dominance.

As we embarked on a trip down the Nile, with a full moon riding high in the heavens, several members told me that they had been on this journey before. As we performed the Sacred Flame

Ritual on the deck of the ship, one woman told me that before taking this trip she had the astral vision that she had been a priestess in the Temple of Isis and Osiris, where she had performed this same ritual many times. The soul's remembrances had brought many of this group on the mystic quest to Egypt to revisit the land of their former glory.

My Own Astral Projection to a Monastery

I once had an astral projection to the ancient land of Tibet, where I saw myself a young monk, about thirty years of age, dressed in a saffron robe, with my head shaved. I walked in a sunlit garden where beautiful flowers bloomed. I sat in a library where I studied books, written not on parchment but on wooden tablets about ten inches long by six inches wide. I read the strange language, which was like Sanskrit, and understood the meaning of what I read.

When I awakened from this astral journey, I wrote down a complete description of what had occurred and drew a picture of the wooden tablets and what they had written on them. The next day I reviewed this astral diary and was amazed at the things it revealed.

At that time, I was lecturing in Carnegie Hall, and it was not until six months later that I had proof that my astral journey to the ancient land of Tibet had been accurate. Reading the *New York Times*, I saw photographs of wooden plaques discovered in a monastery in Tibet, which had been hidden under a mountain landslide three centuries ago! These were the wooden tablets I had seen in my dreams. Scholars of Oriental languages were mystified by the strange writing, which is no longer in existence today.

8. Before going out onto the astral realms in your sleep, you can instruct your soul to enable you to contact the thought entities of the great geniuses of history. If you want to invent something unusual, you can ask to make contact with the souls of men like Thomas A. Edison, Eli Whitney, Cyrus McCormick, or Benjamin Franklin. From one or more of these great men you may be given information that will put you on the path to fame and fortune.

Elias Howe invented the sewing machine through such an astral vision. He had been having a problem getting the needle to carry the thread through the cloth, and he went to bed one night highly discouraged by this obstacle to the completion of his invention. That night he had a vivid astral dream in which he saw Africans carrying spears, but they were not ordinary pointed spears; each one had a hole in its sharp point. When he awoke he knew that his dream was trying to tell him something. He experimented by putting a hole in the needle and threading it. The needle then passed through the cloth, carrying the thread with it perfectly!

Robert Louis Stevenson told of how he had astral projections to strange lands where he met the characters that went into his stories. Even though he was bedridden and could not travel, his soul had astral flights that opened up the entire world to his questing mind. One of Stevenson's greatest stories, *Dr. Jekyll and Mr. Hyde,* was revealed to him while he was on one of his astral journeys as he slept.

9. Before you go out onto the astral while you sleep, you may ask your soul to reveal chemical formulas to you or to let you meet characters that can be put into a great novel; or you may ask for the soul of a Mozart, Chopin, or Beethoven to release heavenly music that you can bring back to earth as musical compositions.

If you wish to become a great industrial genius and found a financial empire, you can tell your soul to contact the thought forms of men like J. P. Morgan, Cornelius Vanderbilt, Aristotle Onassis, and Howard Hughes to help you find your birthright of fame and riches.

Perhaps you want to paint great pictures, and your soul needs inspiration and beauty from the immortals like Michelangelo, Leonardo da Vinci, Thomas Gainsborough, or Rembrandt. Their souls still exist in another dimension of time and space, and these geniuses will help you if you magnetize your mind with the desire to be inspired by them.

10. You may also ask your soul to bring back visions of future events for yourself, your family, your country. These prophetic visions could warn you of impending danger or foretell accurately

the events that might occur in your life, such as moves to another locality, trips you should or should not take, the person you should marry, and many other events scheduled in your cosmic timetable.

A Dream Led This Man to Discover Oil

A man who lived in Oklahoma, in the early days before vast fields of oil were discovered there, needed money to pay off a mortgage on his land. One night he had an astral vision in which he found a big pool of oil on his acreage; it was even pinpointed for him as to its exact location. He had geologists check the area and oil companies bid for leases. They drilled one hole and immediately discovered huge reserves of oil, which made this man enormously rich.

It is noted in history books that before the tragic earthquake that leveled San Francisco in 1906, several people had astral visions in which they saw a severe earthquake hitting the city.

11. When you have completed your astral flights, your soul will automatically return to your earthly body without any need for concern on your part. This process is called Interiorization. You may have a vivid dream in which you are falling through space; and when your soul reenters your body, you may awaken and find yourself shaking, still retaining the vivid sensation of falling. Try to recall all your astral visions, and write them down before you go back to sleep. Some of these dreams will be meaningless to you, but others may hold prophecies, warnings, and symbols of future events that will guide you to the fulfillment of your karmic destiny.

REVIEW OF POINTS IN CHAPTER FOURTEEN

1. A mystical realm exists in the astral where the soul may have experiences while you sleep that are like vivid dreams.
2. The mystics of India, China, Tibet, and Egypt called the soul Divine Essence and ascribed to it properties of the divine, which can know all, see all, and be all on astral planes while we sleep.

3. Joan of Arc had astral visions in which she saw herself leading the armies of France to victory.

4. King Philip of Macedon dreamed of his wife's womb being sealed off with the impression of a lion on the seal. This was a prophecy of the birth of his son Alexander the Great.

5. King Cyrus of Persia, Julius Caesar, and many other famous figures of history had prophetic dreams that foretold their conquests, their sufferings, and even their assassinations.

6. John F. Kennedy had an astral vision of his future assasination.

7. You can use astral projection to reveal future events and set your cosmic time clock by prerecording events of that future on the soul's akashic record.

8. Masters in Tibet have been able to project the astral body and make it visible to people hundreds of miles away.

9. You can instruct your soul to go out into the astral realm while you sleep, giving it instructions to do certain things or to visit certain countries of the past.

10. The soul is able to orbit into its astral realm, where it can contact the souls of others, receive information, and tap secrets of the infinite, which you will later recall.

11. A mystic quest to Egypt with 100 of my students revealed that many of them had previous astral experiences of that ancient land and felt they had been there in other lifetimes.

12. I once had an astral vision of visiting the ancient land of Tibet and reading books written on wooden tablets in a buried monastery. These tablets were later uncovered, and the story was carried in *The New York Times*.

13. Great inventions, ideas for stories and songs, and brilliant ideas, given by geniuses who have gone on before, may come through on your astral journey.

15

COMMON DREAM SYMBOLS TO HELP YOU INTERPRET YOUR DREAMS

In attempting to interpret your own dreams by studying the most common types of symbols that appear in dreams, be aware of the fact that nothing is in your dreams that you did not put there! You own psychic mind is well aware of the reason for clothing the actions of your dreams in these various forms or symbols.

We shall only attempt to give brief interpretations of the most common dreams that occur, as there are far too many thousands of dreams and combinations of symbols to attempt to cover the whole broad range of dream activity.

These dream symbols are listed here in alphabetical order for easy reference.

A

ABORTION Symbolizes fear of childbirth, natural anxiety and fear of pregnancy, or warnings that something may be wrong physically that makes childbearing dangerous.

ACCIDENTS Subconscious fear of mutilation or danger; could be subconscious warnings of automobile accidents, muggings, or attacks on dark streets.

ANGER Arguments, fits of anger, destruction by those who are angry indicate subconscious rebellion against your job, your boss, your in-laws, your mate, or others.

ANIMALS Attacks by ferocious animals indicate warnings of persons who might harm you; also indicate the suppressed and animalistic sexual cravings, which may not be faced consciously. Lions may indicate courage needed to face problems.

B

BELLS Ringing of bells indicates news that might arrive soon. If funereal bells, sad news; if wedding bells or church bells, could be something important or arrival of good news.

BIRDS Flocks of birds making great noise indicate confusion, flights from reality, and desire to leave old life to go into new one. Symbol of desire to be free of restraining forces in love, marriage, or work.

BIRTH Indication that something new is about to be born; creative and inspirational ideas; sexual connotations of pleasure-pain, anxiety, or suppression. If birth is accompanied by pain and difficulties, it may be warning of interference with creative plans.

BITING Biting someone could indicate suppressed rage at someone who represents authority in your life. If animal bites person, indicates fear of encounter with dangerous situation. Being devoured by some elemental force that you fear may symbolize a marriage or a position you hate that is devouring you.

BLOOD Symbolizes life energy or force; could be warning of possible lowering of life energy or of danger to body. Blood of a lamb could symbolize spiritual rebirth or new religious experiences.

BODY Dreams of parts of the body indicate some concern about self; the ego might be having identity problems; if body is sick, subconscious may be warning one to be cautious of diet and to watch one's health. Hiding a body or killing a person could be indicative of attempt to conceal hatred or a subconscious desire to remove some person from life.

BOOKS Indicate desire for acquiring knowledge. Book of life represents fulfillment through studying. If college student dreams of books, could be signs of anxiety at not passing grades. Libraries symbolize the person's hunger for wisdom.

BRIDGE A crossing over to a new life experience, indicating line of demarcation between past and future.

BURIAL If buried alive, indicates anxiety and worry about survival in business, marriage, or health. If another person is buried, may show desire to remove competition or kill off something obnoxious and destructive.

C

CASTRATION Men often have this dream, which indicates hidden fears about their masculinity, fear of women, or concern that they may become impotent.

CATASTROPHE Storms, cyclones, earthquakes, and other forms of disaster could relate to subconscious warnings to protect yourself from future calamity. Also indicates removal of present conditions through turbulence. Divorces, deaths, operations, or other physical forms of danger could be symbolized by dreams of natural or manmade catastrophies.

CEMETERY May represent the burial of hopes and aspirations in a life of futility. Also could relate to wish that you could put past behind you. Resurrection after burial could symbolize the soul's rebirth through a spiritual experience such as religious conversion or being saved.

CLIMBING A mountain or hill represents aspirations to achieve some high goal. If obstacles appear, this indicates the subconscious fears that someone or something may oppose him in his climb to success.

CLOCKS Indicate passage of time or transition from one phase of life to another. Person may be wasting time and this symbol warns that time is money. Person may fear passage of time, age, decline, death.

CLOTHES Being dressed in finery usually indicates pride in accomplishment; if clothes are dirty or torn, shows lack of pride and fear of failure, public disgrace, or exposure. Nakedness indicates concern that one cannot measure up to the world's expectations, or sexual fantasies that might be revealed, bringing the dreamer disgrace and censure.

CROWN Symbols of royalty usually indicate ego struggle. Crown, diadem, royal robes or tiara indicate the person's longing for recognition in his work. May symbolize suppressed fears of financial insecurity and needs to bolster up one's confidence.

D

DANCING If pleasure comes from dreams of dancing, it shows the suppressed desire to express oneself in some creative and artistic way. Painful dancing shows struggle with life situation. Dancing with many partners could indicate desire to change partners in the sex act and have new sexual experiences.

DARK Fear of dark indicates childish fears still existing in the unconscious. Anxiety about work or love life may represent stumbling through life, unable to see the path or where it is leading one. If fearful creatures inhabit the darkness, shows fear of unknown obstacles, problems, and burdens on the path of life.

DEATH Most common dreams of death indicate the person's subconscious fears of this transition, which is shrouded with mystery. The subconscious may be trying to warn the dreamer of death through tragedy. Grief at the death of some loved one shows concern about losing some person, or the stifling of ambition, or the death of one's dream of success.

DESERT Dreams of barren land indicate fear of being sterile and impotent. Also may symbolize futility in one's work or marriage, wasted time and effort, or lack of financial security. May indicate stifling emotions yielding only barrenness and impotence.

DEVIL May result from the two sides of nature, angel and devil, struggling for supremacy; indicates fear of death, going to hell, doing evil acts that require punishment, or self-flagellation over infractions of society's moral codes.

DRUNK Dreams about drinking or drunks tie in with subconscious concern one has for irresponsible acts. May be subconscious warning that debauchery is leading one to ruin, and to go easy on liquor, drugs or cigarettes.

E

EARTH If viewed from distance, indicates a desire to escape into a world of unreality and fantasy. If earth spins like a globe, desire to circle the earth, to travel all over the world.

EARTH-QUAKES Sign of fear of upsetting conditions that could destroy one's work, love life, marriage, or financial situation; tearing down of old structures, building a new destiny.

EATING If gorging to satiety, could be warning of wrong diet or digestive difficulties. If enjoyment results, symbol of sexual satisfaction and fulfillment. If eating glass, foul things, or worms, indicates serious mental disturbances due to worry, fear and anxiety, and possible need for psychiatric help.

EGGS Hatching of eggs indicates new ideas being born; rotten eggs, fear of destruction of dreams; colored eggs, hopes and aspirations representing Easter, rebirth, and regeneration.

ELEPHANTS Docile and friendly elephants indicate the desire to win admiration and friendship of others in the arena of life. If rogue elephant that is destructive and belligerent, shows subconscious fear that one's actions may be destroying the chances for happiness. It may be a subconscious disguise of person who is timid and fearful; if big and powerful like an elephant, he would no longer be self-conscious and feel inferior.

ESCAPING Escape from danger or prison shows desire to get away from a life situation that has become tiring or boring. If complications arise and escape is foiled, this symbolizes a subconscious fear that you are imprisoned by a situation from which there is no escape. Could also be a suppressed suicidal impulse that makes one want to escape from life because it is too painful.

EYEGLASSES If glasses break, indicates subconscious fear of enmity or not being able to see danger ahead. Also could be a subconscious warning to check one's eyes or glasses.

F

FALLING Dreams of falling from great heights indicate subconscious fears of losing out in life, losing money, unhappiness in love or marriage, or the bottom dropping out of one's investments or finances. If flying and then falling, indicates trying to escape from problems but not succeeding. Also may be warning of downfall through bad habits.

FAMILY Dreams about family groups or family members could be subconscious warnings that some person in the family may be in for an illness or unpleasant experience. If the dream is of family dinners or picnics, it indicates a love of family and sharing of love with the family. If a dream of family member dying, could indicate some danger or illness to that person.

FENCES This could represent frustration and futility in one's work or personal life: being "fenced in" and wanting out, hoping to be free from a frustrating situation. A fence could also represent being shut out of life experiences, being an outcast, on the outside looking in but not participating in life's joyous experiences.

FIGHTING If one dreams of fighting some specific person, it could indicate suppressed hostility towards him. If others are fighting, it could indicate two opposing forces struggling for supremacy in the dreamer's mind. If it is a large-scale war, it might indicate the breaking out of hostilities in your personal, business, or social life.

FIRE Dreams of flames or fire are often associated with sexual stimulation: a suppressed desire for some person or a feeling of being consumed with a passion that is not easily fulfilled. Dreams of fire can also be warnings for one to be cautious of fires in the home, to check for faulty wiring, and to have escape ways planned. Fire that destroys one's home or property symbolizes fear of disaster in personal or business life.

FISHING OR FISH Symbolical of underlying, deeper consciousness. Also refers to cold-bloodedness in sexual relations, infertility, or impotence. The fish as a phallic symbol may relate to sexual activity, promiscuity, or uncontrolled sexual impulses. "Poor fish" or "cold fish" are terms often used to designate persons who are hit by misfortune or are sexually cold. Two fish swimming in opposite directions could indicate the dreamer will soon have to make a choice of two courses of action. If the dreamer is fishing and catches nothing, it indicates fear of failure. If there is a good catch, it indicates that one's ventures will meet with success.

FLOODS If the floods are destructive, indicates subconscious fear that one's success is being washed away. May symbolize danger of involvement with destructive forces or persons.

FLOWERS Could indicate that success will bloom in the garden of destiny from the seeds that have been planted in the past. If weed patches make the garden unsightly, could indicate mental carelessness, inefficiency, or wrong planning that blights one's garden. If receiving gifts of bouquets of flowers, indicates that some beautiful experience is about to occur, or that an opportunity will arise for some gratifying experience.

FOG If stumbling through the fog and lost, indicates confusion, mental disorientation, losing one's way, or being in danger of losing money, position, or something else of value. If the fog lifts so that one can see clearly, indicates that the cloudbanks of confusion and disorientation are lifting, giving one the signal to pursue one's goals with success.

FRUIT Indicates the fruit on the tree of life, which can be of various kinds. Also indicates fertility and the harvesting of the crop of abundance in the autumn of life. May foretell some beneficial event bringing fulfillment and growth in business, romance, or social life.

FUNERAL If it is your own funeral, indicates fear of death. Could also be subconscious warning of danger, sickness, or a suppressed fear of death from accident or tragedy. If it is someone else's funeral, shows a desire to remove a person from competition or the life scene.

G

GAMES If you find yourself playing games, as in childhood, could indicate a desire to return to carefree life of the past. If games are pleasant, signifies desire to get more out of the "game of life" and to play more than you work. A person who is overworked and worried often releases his tensions in dreams of playing tennis, golf, baseball, or games of chance, which one wins.

GATE Signifies entrance into new experiences or being shut out of life's more rewarding ventures, depending on whether the gate is open or shut. May symbolize the entrance to a new state of consciousness. May signify psychic centers being opened to reveal future. Entrance to paradise when gates swing open indicates new romantic experiences, expansion of vision, and enlargement of areas of activity in personal or business life.

GHOSTS Refer to the higher mind, relating to "Father, Son, and Holy Ghost" of spiritual experiences. Also indicate the extinction of some formidable opposition, leaving only a ghost image or memory of past problems, opposition, or competition.

GIVING If giving away money, could indicate a desire to help people. Also often refers to losing out in a business venture, giving up, or giving away one's ideas without recompense. If dream persists, could indicate that the psychic mind is trying to warn the dreamer of serious financial losses. If giving friends gifts or other things of value, indicates a generous nature and a secret desire for money and fame so that you can help family and friends.

GOD Dreams of a deity indicate the search for one's higher spiritual identity and what is called Cosmic Consciousness. If it is a God of hellfire and damnation, might indicate a sense of moral guilt, worrying about sexual abuses, or infractions of moral or spiritual laws. If it is a nebulous image of a God hidden by clouds, indicates a mystical experience or a soul search for ultimate cosmic fulfillment.

GUNS A gun has always held significance of a sexual experience, being the phallic symbol of the male organ of fertility. If the gun is being shot, dream has overtones of fear of impotence or infertility, and the person is overly anxious to prove his masculinity. If a crime of violence occurs in which one uses a gun to kill or threaten, it could signify the wish to be the aggressor in the sexual act. It can also indicate fear or worry about being robbed, mugged, or murdered. If the dreamer assaults someone else with a gun, or knife, indicates suppressed hostility towards a person or life situation.

H

HELL Dreams of hell or purgatory signify some hidden fears and anxieties about being punished for moral wrongs, or suppressed sexual fantasies. If one is consumed by flames, can symbolize a purifying process, a purging by fire in which the person is being tested, strengthened, and made pure. Also may relate to a religious experience. If flames engulf the body, could be a warning of a sickness or danger to health and indicate a need for caution in regard to one's health.

HEROES If one dreams of statues of heroes, this could indicate a search for someone to put on a pedestal in your love life. It represents the higher side of your nature, the idealistic, beautiful, and civilized nature rising above the bestial appetites and passions.

HIDING If the dreamer is hiding from an enemy, this shows a subconscious fear of exposure for some illicit act. Subversion or perversion in which the person fears public shame and exposure are often indicated.

HOLE Falling into a deep hole and not being able to get out indicates subconscious warnings that the dreamer is getting in too deep and that some situation threatens to engulf his finances, his business prospects, or his personal life. May suggest caution in gambling, getting into debt, or forming habits that might bury one in the depths of oblivion, poverty, and failure.

HOME Dreams about the home, if pleasant, are childhood memories that the dreamer wishes to renew. It may indicate a search for safety and security. If there are many problems in the dreamer's life, he regresses to his childhood state, where he was secure in the bosom of his family and the sanctity of his home.

HOT Dreams of hot liquids spilling over one or hot water bubbling up from the earth relate to sexual fantasies or the ejaculation of semen; may indicate fertility and growth. Also the "hot" ideas that come through inspiration: creativity, art, music, and literature. If harm comes from the hot liquids, could be warnings to avoid sexual excesses or to go slow on some risky venture that might get one into "hot water."

I

INCEST If one dreams of having sexual relations with a mother, father, or some other member of the family, it can indicate a childhood fixation on one of the parents or suppressed longings for intimate relations with some member of the family, such as a brother, sister, aunt, or uncle.

INDIANS If one dreams of being attacked or wounded by Indians, could indicate suppressed fear of the "arrows of misfortune" that are plaguing you with failure and frustration. Also the rising of subconscious phantoms, due to early childhood fears of danger, authority, and punishment.

INSANITY Dreams that one is going insane or crazy could be warnings of great nervous strain, disorientation, and confusion. Restraints may exist that are "driving you crazy." You may feel that you are in a straitjacket because you are not free to make moves in your chosen direction. Dreams of confinement and restraint indicate subconscious feelings of rebellion, with a desire to make changes.

INSECTS Dreaming of being attacked, bitten, or devoured by hordes of insects could be subconscious warnings of illness. Might also warn that you are being submerged and conquered by negative forces in life. If lice cover your body, it indicates deep anxiety that you are being absorbed by your work, that your marriage is floundering, or that you are being devoured by unfulfilled longings and passion.

ISLAND To be stranded on an island waiting to be rescued indicates loneliness, frustration, or a feeling that one is socially undesirable. May also indicate deep feelings of inferiority and self-consciousness that make one feel an outcast from the normal stream of life. It can also suggest a secret desire to get away from a problem, a job, or a marriage, and to literally be alone on some distant island where there is peace and security.

J

JEALOUSY If the dreamer finds himself filled with jealous rage, it could indicate he is suppressing jealousy for his beloved. Also signifies dislike of some person opposing one or someone who is in a superior position. Jealousy usually relates to the primitive emotions of resentment, hate, and a desire to kill one's opposition.

JEWELS Rubies, diamonds, emeralds, and pearls often represent things that are precious to the dreamer. A jewel can be a symbol for some person that one loves dearly, or it can be a symbol of something valuable that will come to the dreamer. Diamonds in a dream indicate the inner or higher self, radiating its splendor and beauty in one's personality; could stand for a valuable experience that is about to occur, or a "jewel of a person" who may grace the dreamer's life and bring gifts of love, kindness, and gentility. Crowns with glittering jewels indicate the achievement of success in some venture that will bring advancement, fortune, fame, and world acclaim—the "crowning achievement" of one's life, so to speak.

JOURNEYS If travel occurs in one's dreams, it can mean a suppressed longing to get away from the boredom of life and to expand one's horizons of experience.

K

KEYS Keys are symbols of a desire to open new doors to opportunity, or they could be a subconscious warning to keep your possessions under lock and key because there may be a robbery. The key has long been a dream symbol of power and of opening locked areas of the mind through consciousness expansion and attainment of knowledge.

KILLING Dreams in which one kills a person could signify a desire to be rid of someone who is standing in his way of success or fulfillment. If the dreamer is being killed by an opponent, it shows fears and anxieties about the safety of his life and fear of death. If the killing is done on a field of battle, the dreamer has suppressed his rage and wants the destruction of his enemies. If the killing is of someone the dreamer loves, it could indicate a desire to get rid of the bad side of the lover's character that is annoying the dreamer.

KISSES To dream of kissing or being kissed by someone you love indicates sexual fulfillment and happiness. If kisses are spurned or being forced on you by someone you dislike, could indicate a broken romance or some disappointment in love or marriage.

KITES Represent soaring dreams and aspirations; a longing to be free of earthbound worries and anxieties.

Also relate to the inspiration to soar to great heights of achievement; lifting of spirits through joyous sexual experiences with one's beloved. Or it may reflect one's need to be free of personal involvements, or of the habits that hold one to a life of futility and failure.

KNIVES Represent the cutting of the umbilical cord that holds one tied to some frustrating situation. Also stand for subconscious desire to carve out one's destiny and to achieve success. A knife in the hands of an adversary could be a warning of personal danger through an assault.

L

LADDER Climbing a ladder symbolizes the ladder of success and the achievement of riches. Also shows the yearnings of the soul to rise above the limitations of earth. If falling off a ladder, indicates danger of losses of money, social position, or business opportunities.

LANGUAGES Speaking fluently in another language could show confusion of identity, misunderstandings with those who are close to you, or garbled messages that lead to error and mistakes. Might also indicate you should study another language to prepare yourself for travel.

LETTERS Receiving a letter with good news often means that something of value may come through the mail. A letter also indicates any kind of message that brings news of importance. If it is edged in black, could be sign of misfortune or of death of someone you know. May also indicate communication with subconscious, releasing great ideas that will inspire and uplift you.

LIGHT To see bright flashes of light, like lightning, or other celestial phenomena might indicate inner illumination or flashes of inspiration. Sometimes indicates that psychic powers are unfolding, leading to ESP experiences. Often related to the person's spiritual illumination or enlightenment in other dimensions of mind and spirit.

LUGGAGE Packing bags for a trip shows a suppressed desire to move "bag and baggage" to get out of some undesirable situation. Also might relate literally to a trip one is about to take, or could indicate preparation to move to another home or business location.

M

MACHINES To dream of machines operating could indicate a restless desire to make some changes in your life. It could also indicate tremendous creative activity on the artistic plane. If the machines are automatic, like computers, this could indicate that your subconscious should be reprogrammed with positive forces. Machines breaking down could mean warnings of bodily sickness or mental disorders.

MASKS To dream of wearing a mask or of others wearing masks indicates a subconscious desire for concealment; it might also warn of treachery or deceit on the part of other persons and warn you to be cautious in affairs of the heart, where some person may hurt you.

MICE To dream of mice or small crawling creatures could indicate subconscious fears eating away at the mind. These relate to personal life, insecurity, and emotional upsets in love and marriage. If a cat kills a mouse, it could indicate that you will triumph over the obstacles and achieve success.

MIRRORS Indicate a duality in the inner and outer selves; you may be two minds in one body, each struggling for supremacy. Might also show pride, vanity, and narcissism, in which the ego requires constant adoration and affection. Could also signify a warning to beware of a two-faced person who might be treacherous.

MONEY Dreams of finding money usually show anxiety about money, bills, problems relating to a mortgage or other debts; shows the subconscious desire to find money to meet your bills. Such a dream also can be prophetic, trying to tell you that money is on the way; shortly thereafter you may receive money through the mail or in an unexpected manner. To dream of losing money shows that you may be careless, may be taking on debts that you cannot afford, or should not loan money or take risks with money.

MONSTERS To dream of horrifying monsters threatening you could signify subconscious fears of danger or threats against health, life, and happiness. Might be warnings that your life is peopled with those who are destructive or cautioning you to be careful of bad habits that could destroy you.

MOON The full moon often indicates a period of great energy, artistic and creative work, and the use of the imagination. The moon stands for the feminine elements and romance; could indicate romantic changes or fulfillment of your ambitions. The full moon is a time when many neurotics and psychotics undergo unusual mental activity, and a dream of one may be a warning to live more in the world of reality and not avoid life's problems.

MOUNTAINS Dreams about mountains indicate the struggle of your higher mind to rise above the limitations of your present job or situation in life and to soar to higher realms of achievement. If you are climbing a mountain and are fearful of falling, it could indicate that there will be problems to face on your upward climb to success and you should be cautious in taking chances.

N

NIGHTMARE To dream you are having a nightmare and are not able to awaken or to scream out for help indicates a very troubled psychic state of mind in which burdens and problems are so heavy your psyche seeks relief in such vivid nightmares.

NUDITY To dream of being naked in public, when others have their clothes on, indicates a desire to shake off conventions and inhibitions relating to sex, a desire to be more promiscuous. Also may indicate that the person is tired of putting on the same pretense each day and desires freedom from restraints that bind him to convention.

NUMBERS To dream of numbers indicates a mathematical mind and might also show lucky numbers, lucky days, or events that are to occur in some future month or year. Many people have dreamed lucky numbers playing at the races, and some have won big lotteries by having dreams of the winning numbers.

NUMBNESS To dream of being numb in certain parts of the body could be a subconscious warning that illness may afflict one through lack of proper circulation. Also indicates emotional shock or some disturbance that will strike, making one numb with grief or shock.

O

OBSTACLES Dreams in which you are trying to reach some goal or climb to some height and obstacles are put in your path indicate that you are experiencing many obstructions to the fulfillment of your dreams. They could also be psychic warnings of danger, suggesting that you should change your plans and take another course of action to reach your goals.

OCCUPATIONS Such dreams often indicate the work you should follow. If it is contrary to the occupation you now have, give it some thought to see if you would benefit by a change.

OLD PEOPLE If of an old man, signifies time, Father Time robbing you of youth, a fear of growing old. Also might suggest your childhood with mother, father, and grandparents being recalled by the subconscious to give feelings of security.

ONIONS This dream has social overtones, as onions give bad breath; could indicate concern as to whether the dreamer is being effective socially. Might also be warning of some sadness to come, as peeling onions often brings tears.

ORGAN To dream of organ music could be sign of your luck changing for the better or a happy event about to befall you.

ORPHANS To dream of orphans could mean some negative experience to come in which you will be robbed of something. Being without parents could also indicate being shorn of happiness or losing out in life and finding yourself alone and friendless.

P

PASSPORT Indicates a subconscious desire to travel to foreign lands, to broaden one's experiences. May also be a sign that the person will soon be given a "passport to paradise" through some exciting new sexual experience or a "passport to fame and fortune" through a new business venture.

PHALLUS Dreams that include symbols of the male or female reproductive organ indicate growth, creativity, and sexual activity in some way. Phallic symbols, such as swords, pens, pencils, bananas, or statues are tied in with the subconscious's suppressed desires, dream fantasies of wanting another lover, or fulfilling one's own dreams in love or marriage.

PREGNANCY For a woman, this dream often indicates a desire to give birth to a child. Or if there is fear in the dream, it might represent a fear of pregnancy and a wish to avoid it. In a man, the dream could indicate suppressed homosexual longings, a desire to change roles and become a woman.

PRISON To dream that one is languishing in prison indicates the subconscious feeling that one's job or marriage in some way has become a prison from which the dreamer wants to escape.

R

RABBITS Changes in location are indicated by this dream, getting about from one place to another with speed. Also, as rabbits breed rapidly, could indicate growth in business and an increase in money and investments.

RAIN To dream of falling rain indicates fertility, productivity, creative action that will bring forth new ideas and riches. This is a good symbol, for it shows the subconscious is trying to reveal how one may make the seeds of thought mature into a crop of riches and abundance.

RAINBOW All the colors of a rainbow suggest the full spectrum of life's experiences and activities. A rainbow is a sign of good luck; finding a "pot of gold at the end of the rainbow." An indication that after the turbulence and storms of life, one will have a period of relief and good fortune.

RAVEN This is supposed to show sadness or impending doom. However, in modern interpretation of dreams, it could also indicate that even though the raven of misfortune hovers over all of us in ultimate death, it could be a symbol of life after death and of new hopes and dreams that arise after the black pall of oblivion and disaster has lifted.

RESCUE To be rescued from a burning ship or from a dangerous situation might warn of some danger ahead and advise caution. May also show that relief is coming in some matter that is causing one concern. It is a good symbol if the rescue is successful and without bad aftereffects.

RICE This symbolizes marriage but also fertility and life—new life in the birth of a child or the outcome of a marriage. If the rice is growing as a crop, indicates that the seedlings of reality will mature into an abundant harvest of everything that is good and beautiful.

RIVER Dreams of a river, winding its way into the distance, or crossing a river could indicate anxiety about problems and a desire for escape. If the crossing is without danger, it indicates that you will be able to cross over this troubled period of life into a more productive and happy life experience.

S

SCHOOL To dream of being in school shows suppressed longings to get away from present problems and return to the carefree, happy days of childhood. Also may symbolize a psychic urge to seek out knowledge or study to prepare for a new career. Represents a period of expansion and growth.

SEXUAL FANTASIES If you find yourself involved in sexual acts that are pleasant, this is a normal and safe type of sexual dream. If, however, there are disturbing elements in the dreams and you suffer shame, pain, or abandonment while performing the sex act, this could be a warning that you are suffering from guilt and should straighten out your mental attitude towards sex. Or it could mean unsatisfied longings that require adjustments with your sexual partner.

SKY A blue sky is indicative of fair times ahead; a gray or stormy sky could be a warning of troubles to come. If the sun is shining in a bright blue sky, this is a good omen and your psychic twin is telling you that you face a period of good luck and good fortune.

SNAKES Frequent dreams of snakes do not mean, as Freud thought, a preoccupation with sex, and snakes are not to be thought of as always representing the phallic symbol for the male organ. It is true that sometimes they represent sexual matters. Snakes usually indicate a person's submerged fears and anxieties. A coiled snake, about to strike, means that you fear that you are reaching a breaking point and are tense and unable to unwind. It is significant also if the floor or ground is covered with writhing snakes and you must thread your way among them to reach some objective. This indicates the subconscious fear that your journey to reach your goals is fraught with danger and that threats continually occur that could keep you from reaching your goals financially, socially, or romantically. If you kill snakes, this means conquest over your fears, vanquishing your enemies, and overcoming your problems.

STARS Seeing stars in your dreams is a good-luck omen, and shows high idealism and the reaching of desirable goals.

STORMS Gales, thunder and lightning, and falling rain are all indications of mental and emotional turbulence. Your psychic twin is trying to warn you that there are hidden problems and dangers that you must avoid.

SURGERY If you dream that you are undergoing surgery, this could be a subconscious warning of health hazards in your present diet and way of life. Also may indicate the removal of something threatening your progress or survival, a cutting off from present situations, or the removal of an inflammatory condition, such as a bothersome person at work or in your home.

T

TEETH A frequent dream is one in which all the teeth fall out, usually accompanied by feelings of horror. This was taken by Freud to mean sexual frustration but modern research shows it to indicate subconscious fear of losing something of value. It could also mean loss of friends, money, or position. As the smile shows a person's friendliness, loss of teeth could mean the loss of friends or that scandal or gossip is robbing one of friends and social acceptance.

TELEPHONE Indicates messages that could come by phone or letter. If the dream is of bad news, could show states of anxiety and fear about failure in life. Also suggests subconscious desire to communicate with others, to be in public work, using the voice, teaching, acting, singing, or preaching.

TREASURE To dream of finding buried treasure or gold, silver, oil, or uranium indicates fear of poverty and subconscious longing for financial security. It could also suggest hidden gifts and talents that might bring a fortune if they are unearthed. Sometimes it relates to the finding of a new love that is more precious than silver or gold. If the treasure eludes one after searching or digging, it means disappointments are on the way and one's wishes and expectations will fail.

TREES To dream of trees is good luck; of being lost in a forest suggests problems that never seem to end. May indicate fertility and growth, especially if trees are laden with fruit.

TUNNEL Dreams of one going through a tunnel and not being able to see the light indicate deep mental conflict, emotional confusion, and disorientation. If there is light at the end of the tunnel, it means the ending of a cycle of misfortune and losses, the finding of the light. Of course, the obvious Freudian interpretation is of a womb and has sexual overtones.

U

UNDERGARMENTS Symbolical of being stripped or undressed; could indicate moral guilt connected with sex or fear of unhappiness in love and marriage. If it is of undressing down to one's underwear, shows one being stripped of fortune, losing a job, or losing a loved one through separation or death. Sometimes denotes losing authority or being stripped of power and demoted to a lower station in life.

UNDER-GROWTH To become tangled in undergrowth or shrubs indicates a mental dilemma, such as a money problem, a romantic matter that is difficult to solve, or some person entangling one in a troublesome emotional alliance.

UTERUS In women, shows some concern about problems relating to pregnancy, childbirth, or menstruation. May also indicate blocked exits and not knowing where to turn to get away from one's problems, frustrations, and fears.

V

VAMPIRES Dreams of flying objects, such as vampires, birds, or winged beasts, that threaten to attack one indicate deep concern about one's future safety and security. Also could be warnings of hidden dangers or of a situation that drains one of his life energy or force (literally having the "blood sucked from him"). Or his job may be bleeding him, in that he does not receive adequate compensation.

VAULTS If you dream of vaults filled with money, jewels, and valuable papers, this could indicate worry and concern about losses through theft, fire, or carelessness. Freud, as usual, saw this as a symbol of the female organs, and ascribed it to various suppressed sexual desires.

VEGETABLES Dreams of a garden filled with vegetables indicate fertility or growth of one's business or plans. If there are weed patches and the vegetables are sparse and few, it is a warning that one's present course of actions may result in loss of money or of business opportunity.

VIOLIN Usually indicates harmonious relationships with members of the opposite sex, "making sweet music together." The male is the bow, the female is the fiddle, and the caressing motion of the bow over the fiddle speaks of a desire for sexual peace and fulfillment.

W

WASHING This is tied in strongly to a desire to cleanse one's mind and soul of some secret guilt. If there are bloodstains that won't come off, in a woman's case they relate to a fear of pregnancy or difficulties in labor and childbirth. In a man, they might indicate that he is trying to remove some mental blotch, or that he fears becoming impotent and thus unable to function sexually.

WATER Dreaming of water has spiritual connotations, for water is the symbol of baptism. May signify a rebirth, letting die the old way of life and entering into a new experience, new work, or a new love affair or marriage.

WEDDING Dreams do not always go by opposites, so a dream of a wedding does not necessarily signify a life of single bliss. Such a dream generally shows some concern about marriage; if married, it could indicate desire for freedom or a new try at marriage. If single, it may be urging the person to marry and settle down.

WERE-WOLVES To dream of humans turning into animals, such as werewolves, bats, horses, or vampires, signifies complex and involved thoughts regarding courses of action to take. May also indicate a duality in one's personality. It may be a warning that some "wolf in sheep's clothing" will deceive one.

WHALE Signifies ambition to achieve greatness, fame, and fortune. As Jonah and the whale are in the mass consciousness, it often indicates that a miracle is about to occur in the dreamer's life, bringing him health, romance, money, or other things of value. It is a good-luck symbol except to sailors, who feel it is bad luck. A white whale symbolizes spiritual purity.

WHEEL The turning of a wheel signifies progress; in machines, it could indicate that the wheels of the mind are turning with creative ideas. It also signifies journeys to distant places or moves of home or business to another locality.

WOMB A dream of the womb or of returning to the womb and being reborn relates to the subconscious desire to return to the state of childhood, free of all problems and concerns. It also has sexual overtones, as Freud pointed out; he gave many symbols for the womb, including small boxes, ovens, chests, vaults, ships, and gardens.

WOUNDS If wounded in battle or by a sharp instrument, could be a warning that warring forces within you may be leading to pyschosomatic illnesses, accidents, or emotional upheavals.

X

X-RAY Dreaming of being X-rayed could show worry and concern, especially in a woman dreaming of breast X-ray, subconscious anxiety that one might have cancer. Also indicates passing experiences that throw a brief picture on the psychic screen of the mind but are not of a permanent nature; all that is short-lived and of a transient nature.

XYLOPHONE To dream of this musical instrument indicates a desire to be in harmony with those about one. If the keys fly off when the hammer hits them, could indicate a period of trouble ahead, discord, and stormy relations as could music that is out of tune, harsh, and discordant.

Y

YACHT Reflects a subconscious desire to escape to other areas of action, or boredom with one's life and work. A symbol of luxury, fortune, and leisure that suggests ambition and desire to rise in life.

YOUNG To dream you are once again young, or have returned to scenes of your childhood, shows a desire to escape from the cares of today to a past era of nostalgia and freedom from concern and worry. If one has a face lift in a dream to become young again, it could show a fear of age and concern about losing one's sexual attractiveness.

Z

ZIGZAG To dream of following a zigzag course that leads to a confused maze without end shows a very troubled mind with possibility of nervous breakdown. May indicate a course in life that has been futile and has led nowhere or subconscious fear of failure and lack of fulfillment.

ZIPPER If you dream of trying to zip up a dress and have difficulties, it indicates romantic involvements that you are not happy about. A desire to change the raiment of your personal life, a marriage or love affair that no longer fits. If hopelessly tangled in the clothing, as in a man's trousers, could be suppressed desires for forbidden sexual promiscuity. Also may indicate a secret fear of losing one's masculinity through castration or other forms of phallic mutilation.

ZOO To dream of many animals, as in a zoo, could signify the suppressed and often hostile elements in one's nature. Or could represent the bestial side of one's personality that has to be suppressed: a desire to give in to inhibitions and indulge in sexual experiences one normally frowns upon; the uncontrolled appetites and passions that lead to licentiousness and eventual mental, moral, and spiritual breakdown.